Indoor Vegetable Gardening

The Ultimate Guide for Beginners Wanting to Grow Organic Vegetables at Home, in the Kitchen, or in Other Places Indoors

Contents

Introduction

Can you grow vegetables indoors? The obvious answer to this question is a resounding "Yes!" Given the right conditions, you can grow many different types of vegetables in your indoor space. From leafy greens to root crops, trees, and herbs, there's practically no limit to what you can grow in your indoor space. Of course, the keyword here is "conditions." The secret of successful indoor gardening is to know how to alter your indoor conditions to suit the needs of your vegetables.

This is easy since indoor gardening ultimately gives you control over every aspect of your plants' growth. You are in the driver's seat and not at the mercy of the outdoor weather conditions or all the critters running around outside. You can control and maintain the right amount of water and nutrient supply, and learn to choose a quality soil that your plants will thrive in.

But with great power comes great responsibility. Growing your vegetables indoors does have its unique challenges. You will learn all about them in this book, and how to solve all the problems you are likely to encounter with your indoor garden. We'll start from the basics and work our way up to the more complex aspects of growing your fruit, herbs, and vegetables indoors. Are you ready? Read on to learn all about growing different types of vegetables and how to have access to a fresh supply of the foods you need in the comfort of your own home at various times throughout the year.

Chapter 1: The Benefits of Gardening Indoors

One of the good things about indoor gardening is that having limited space is not a barrier. You don't need acres of land, nor do you need to build a greenhouse. With nothing more than a sunny windowsill in your apartment, you can plant and tend your garden and still enjoy the benefits of gardening regardless of the size of the garden space available.

Gardening indoors may be a matter of necessity (a city dweller without a backyard space may have to plant a garden indoors) or just due to personal preferences for its many benefits. No matter your reasons, gardening indoors is not an easy feat.

Benefits of Indoor Gardening

Gardening itself can be refreshing, with a lot of benefits to your physical and mental health. The process of weeding, raking, watering, and tending your plants can help you relax and relieve stress.

But why do people opt to do it indoors? Aside from the obvious reason that an indoor garden provides you with fresh, non-contaminated produce, there are plenty of other benefits to gardening indoors. The following are some of the benefits of indoor gardening.

Climate Control

Outdoor gardeners know that the saying "Nature knows best" doesn't always hold true. Like fire, nature is a kind servant but a harsh master. You have limited control over the outdoor climate. While it is true that plants need a lot of water and sunlight to grow, all of which may be abundant in an outdoor environment, nature can overdo things sometimes.

Garden plants are delicate and can be affected by the excess of any natural element. It is almost impossible to control growing conditions outdoors, and it's a lot easier when your garden is indoors. In the same way, we can tweak our indoor environment to suit ourselves, so it doesn't get too hot, too cold, or too humid. You can also do the same for your indoor plants.

An indoor gardening system allows you to control the amount of light, water, and nutrients your plants get at any time of the day. Even if harsh and unstable weather conditions don't affect your plants, you can't tend the plants when it's drizzling or cold outside. Having your garden indoors means you can access your plants whenever you need to without worrying about catching a cold or getting your shoes wet.

Pests

Anyone who has ever attempted to grow an outdoor garden will tell you that there's a constant battle between them and pests, from adorable bunnies that dig out plant roots to those pesky insects that can destroy entire plants within a few days. There are birds and rodents to contend with, all of which can make outdoor gardening more than a tad frustrating. After all your hard work, you may never get to eat the food you grow in your garden because the pests got to them before you did.

Of course, there are several ways to keep the pests away from your outdoor garden. Still, indoor planting is a low-maintenance and low-cost option, especially if you want to avoid the stress of creating a pest-proof barrier in the yard or you'd prefer not to use chemicals on your plants.

That's not to say that indoor plants are entirely pest-free. Some insect pests still find their way inside your home and may affect your plants. Your cat or dog could knock your garden pots over if you are also a pet parent. But you have better control over these than you would with a garden where everything is out in the open.

Space

In some cases, gardening indoors is the only option you have if you want to garden at all. This is particularly true for people who live in an urban setting where it may be impossible to find space to grow your plants outside. A lack of backyard space, patio, or balcony means gardening indoors is your only chance to grow your own plants.

An indoor gardener need not worry about a lack of indoor space. You can grow vegetables and herbs right in your kitchen, in the corner of your living room, or on your windowsills. Even in tiny homes, you may still be able to accommodate dozens of indoor plants by growing them vertically. The possibility of using grow-lights means your plants don't necessarily need access to a window or natural light, which means you can grow them pretty much anywhere you find space for them in your home.

Getting Your Kids Involved

One of the benefits of growing plants in a climate-controlled environment is that it is less stressful and easier to get your kids involved with gardening. Collaborating on tending your indoor garden with your kids not only provides a way to bond with them but also helps them to start learning about plants and gardening from an early age. They will learn how the right amount of light, moisture, and nutrients aid plant growth.

Having a little experimental garden indoors like this can also prepare your kids for a larger-scale outdoor garden. This will spark their curiosity and interest in gardening as it serves as a sort of introduction to gardening in general.

Indoor Gardening Purifies the Air

You probably remember from your introductory biology class that plants breathe the opposite of how people do. The natural process through which plants produce the energy they need for growth uses water and carbon dioxide. A byproduct of this process is oxygen. Indoor plants act as natural purifiers that remove excess carbon dioxide from your space while introducing fresh oxygen into your home.

What's more, certain plants take this a step further. They don't just circulate oxygen and carbon dioxide, but they can also filter dust, germs, and toxins out of the air. Examples of such plants include snake plants, English ivy, chrysanthemums, and spider plants.

Attractive Décor

If you check online, you'll probably find plenty of Pinterest pages dedicated to indoor garden décor. A gorgeous blooming flower or even a large leafy plant can transform an indoor space. There are a lot of creative ways to transform the appearance of your space using plants. Cactus gardens, windowsills of blooming flowers, and beautiful succulent arrangements can transform your space and create a pleasing environment that looks good and feels good. It's a healthier and more vibrant environment that also looks great in Instagram photos.

Convenience

Most people don't grow the plants outdoors because of all the stress involved. The truth is, gardening outside can be quite a chore. You need to dig the dirt, pull weeds, water your plants, and do a wide range of other maintenance processes. All of this is not a problem for someone who does gardening as a hobby. You may even find all of these activities therapeutic and fun.

But not everyone sees gardening in this way. You may not think going to war with pests or tilling the ground is all fun and games. You may also not have enough time on your hands for all of these activities. Although it still takes some work to tend to your indoor plants, indoor gardening is less physically demanding than planting outdoors.

Extended Growing Season

I have mentioned how climate conditions fluctuate erratically and how this can affect the growth of your indoor plants. Another consequence of planting outdoors is that weather conditions vary by season. This limits what you can plant at any given time. A controlled indoor environment eliminates the time restrictions of the seasons.

You can begin growing seedlings ahead of the growing season, grow plants out of their regular growing season, or continue growing even after the regular growing season has finished. The space in your house is entirely under your control. You can adjust the light, temperature, and water conditions to mimic any condition you intend to replicate much more easily than you could in an outdoor space.

Emotional Therapy

Indoor plants can be treated with the same care as you give your pets. They share the same space with you and rely on your care and attention to cater to their needs. Tending to your indoor garden requires a great sense of compassion. Some people even talk to their plants like they would to their puppy. Life is less lonely and more enjoyable when you have to prune, water, repot, and carry out other tasks related to caring for your indoor garden. It is believed that indoor gardening can reduce the risk of depression and create a sense of satisfaction. Indoor gardening is recommended to improve your physical and emotional wellbeing.

Different Types of Indoor Garden Space

A lot has been said about how indoor gardening is a simple and more convenient way to grow plants. But that's not to say you don't need to pay attention to your indoor growing environment. As you will discover during the course of this book, there are very clear differences between gardening outdoor and indoors. You must adapt your gardening style to create the environment that will be most suitable for your plants.

So, how do you get the most from your indoor plants? The starting point will be what you want your indoor garden to look like. Houseplants can be planted in different ways and placed in different parts of your home.

To get the best results from your indoor gardening, you will need to create an environment in your home as close to the plants' natural habitat as possible. This begins with where you place the plants and the type of conditions you expose them to.

Which Rooms Work Best?

Like all plants, houseplants need sunshine. They're affected by temperature, humidity, and a whole host of other natural conditions. Of course, each plant will differ in terms of what they need. But there are basic requirements you should pay attention to.

Indoor plants cannot just be positioned anywhere, thoughtlessly. Your plant is a living thing rather than just part of your décor. Thus, the goal isn't just fancy placement or growing a garden in the spot where you think it will have the most aesthetic value. You still have to do what's best for your plants.

To determine proper plant placement, you need to consider factors such as light conditions, the direction of your windows, the position of your heaters, the average temperature of the house, and the temperature of specific rooms, among other factors. Putting all of these together will help you determine the best areas to place your houseplants.

Houseplants are just as varied in diversity as outdoor plants. Every plant you grow in your indoor garden needs light in some form. But while some plants will thrive more when there's an abundant supply of light, others will perform better under partial or full shade conditions.

The type of plants in your indoor garden will determine where you plant your garden and what your garden will look like. Light-loving plants are best positioned at a north-facing or south-facing window, depending on the latitude and season. (The angle of the sun's daily arc through the sky, or "declination", varies with the seasons; plus, its angle of declination in the northern hemisphere is the opposite of that seen in the southern hemisphere, using the equator as the dividing line. A basement window may yield full sunlight from late spring through early autumn, but that same window is shaded by the house the rest of the year, when it needs to be admitting direct sunlight the most.)

But most other plants will be good with windows facing east or west.

For instance, foliage and flowering plants like ferns and lilies will do well with minimal sunlight and easily grow with artificial lighting. Plants like this are ideally placed some feet away from a window facing the sun. They can be placed closer to an east-or-west-facing window, but so as to keep them out of the midday sun.

Similarly, plants with thick and fleshy leaves like Jade, Zebra plant, and Stonecrop do well in the shade, and you can keep them out of the sun for the most part.

Upcycled Seed Pots

You don't necessarily need a fancy seed tray or plant pot to grow your plants. There is a chance that there are containers in your home right now that can be upcycled into a seed tray to grow your plants in.

You can use an old ice cube tray, empty yogurt containers, or Styrofoam cups as seed planters, repotting later as your plant grows.

Newspaper or Toilet Paper Roll

For those that prefer to use something more biodegradable to plant their seeds, folded newspaper or toilet paper rolls can be repurposed into seed planters. The newspaper can be folded into an open box shape or a cup. You can make two shallow cuts at one end of a toilet paper roll and fold it up in a canister shape that allows you to put soil in it.

Egg Carton Planter

Another popular form of commonly upcycled material used for planting seeds is old egg cartons. You can cut these cartons into any size to create seed farms for your garden plants. You can also put soil in empty eggshells and plant seeds in them. The plants can use the calcium and other minerals from the eggshell as it grows.

One major advantage of starting your indoor garden with seeds planted in biodegradable materials like eggshells and cardboard is that they can be planted directly into the soil when it's time to replant the seedlings into a larger pot. The materials will break down, and the roots can grow directly into the soil.

Indoor Gardening with Plastic Bottles

Plastic bottles can be used to make seed planters, which is a good thing because it will make use of waste plastic which is bad for the environment. They are not biodegradable, and they pollute the land and water when discarded carelessly. But you can put them to excellent use in your indoor garden instead of throwing them out.

The bottles can be cut easily using a pair of scissors or a kitchen knife. A hole is cut in the side of the bottle, fresh soil poured in, and the seed or seedling transferred into it. Plastic bottle gardens make a perfect display spot. A few can be secured together with strings or joined with zip ties, then strung on a wire frame to create a vertical garden.

Tin Can Garden

Another planting-pot alternative for your indoor garden is using old cans. You should clean them before planting your seeds in them. Even better, the cans can be painted or decorated to match your interior décor.

You can create a small windowsill garden with fresh plants grown out of tin cans of different sizes. This creates an aesthetically appealing and perfectly rustic look. Alternatively, you can drill a hole in the edge of each can and suspend them with hooks on an open wall or over the kitchen sink.

Vertical Gardens with Shoe Organizers

Vertical gardens save space. So, even if you don't have a lot of space to spare because your apartment is small, you can still create a suspended garden for your plants. One of the ways to do this is by converting your old shoe organizer into an indoor garden. You can hang the shoe organizer on a wall with good sunlight and fill each pocket with a mixture of pebbles and dirt. Each pocket should be lined with a plastic grocery bag to prevent water from draining onto the floor. Flowers, vegetables, and various types of herbs can be grown in this way.

Fish Tank Terrarium

If you have an empty fish tank just lying around, you could make good use of it by converting it into an indoor garden. You can also buy a simple fish tank at a meager price if you love the look of an aquarium garden. They make the perfect makeshift greenhouses for plants and seedlings. An extra advantage of using a fish tank to host your plants is that it can be covered with a transparent plastic lid or a plastic wrap to keep the pests out and control humidity.

Fish tank terrariums can be used for seedlings as well as fully-grown plants. They are most suitable for mosses, succulents, and some decorative plants.

Factors new indoor gardeners should take into consideration when choosing an indoor space for plants

An indoor garden is a low-maintenance way to grow plants. But that does not let you off the hook as far as planning your garden is concerned. If anything, growing plants indoors requires some special considerations and planning. There are different types of garden room ideas you can explore, which is why you need to sit down and consider your options to determine what will give you the best results. These are some things you need to keep in mind if you are planning to start an indoor garden.

Choosing a Location

Whether you are dedicating an entire room or a small area to your indoor garden, there are many factors to consider regarding the location. This will probably prove to be the most crucial indoor gardening decision you'll make. There is a lot to consider, including:

- How much light is available, and if you'll be needing supplementary light

- The natural temperature of the room, and if heat will need to be added

- How temperature, humidity, and other factors vary with the season

The good thing about indoor gardening is that many of these factors are within your control. If you have a warm toasty room that receives no sunlight, artificial light can fix this. Conversely, if the room gets good sun exposure but the temperature isn't optimal, you can fix this with an ordinary heater. You just need to be aware of what you need to change and adjust to suit your plants.

Outfitting the Room

Growing indoor plants for most people means they have to design their natural living space to accommodate the plants. This means adjusting the heat and humidity factors to those comfortable for you and still suitable for your plant. Unless you are dedicating an entire room to gardening, in which case the room's atmospheric factors can be tailored to suit your plants, this is often a somewhat difficult balance to achieve perfectly. To transform your space into a conducive space for plants, here are some things you will have to alter:

- **Your Flooring:** Wooden or carpet flooring doesn't go well with indoor gardening, as water can easily stain or damage it. Great garden floor ideas include ceramic, linoleum, or slate.

- **Lighting:** Plants need the optimal amount of light to grow properly. So even if your home has sufficient lighting for you, there's a good chance you'll need more for your plants, especially during certain seasons of the year. You may need to add some broad-spectrum lights or fluorescent lighting to your space.

- **The Airflow:** Good ventilation is necessary for proper plant growth. You can consider adding a floor or ceiling fan to your space if the room is not well ventilated. Proper ventilation is not only good for your plants but also ensures that you are comfortable in your space as well.

- **Humidity:** The humidity level has to be at an optimal level. You can install a humidifier with a timer feature to add more humidity to the room if necessary.

Choose the Plants

Choosing your indoor garden plants depends on several factors, which include:

- The purpose of gardening - do you want decorative plants, or are you planting for food and/or herbs?
- The type of décor you are going for
- How much space do you have?
- The condition of your indoor space

If you are planting a high-light plant such as a citrus plant or gardenias, you have to be prepared to create sufficient light by supplementing natural light with close artificial lights. Even for low-light plants like philodendron or other types of palms, you will need to create a tropical feel for your plant room. You can either choose a plant that is suited to survive in the type of space you can provide or take steps to alter the condition of your space to suit the plant you intend to grow in your garden.

You should also keep in mind that some garden plants don't grow well together. For instance, if you are growing an herb garden, you have to isolate mint from the rest of your plants. Mint grows wildly and may kill off other plants in your garden.

Selecting plants that go together will also ensure a balance of light, water, and nutrient conditions. There's only so much variety you can create when it comes to natural habitats for different plants. A good practice is to choose plant varieties that have the same or very similar requirements for sunlight and soil conditions. Rosemary and cilantro cannot be planted together because the latter requires more moisture. A better combination with rosemary would be sage or lavender.

Select an Indoor Garden Design

You can settle on a garden design after selecting your garden plants and figuring out all the modifications you may need to make. There are plenty of indoor garden design ideas and themes you can explore. Picking a theme or specific design ensures that your indoor garden is not all over the place, disorganized, or even distasteful.

Space Is Important

In addition to picking a design, you also have to consider the size of your space. While it is true that you can have a garden indoors even with limited space, you still have to be thoughtful about it. Your garden space should be as clutter-free and accessible as possible, or it will be harder for you to get to the plants. As I mentioned earlier, suspending your garden on a wall or growing it on a windowsill is a great option when you don't have enough space on the floor for the plants.

The "less is more" principle couldn't be more accurate when it comes to indoor gardening. Planting too many things into too small a space will mean having to squash the plants together. They just won't grow as great as they should. Your plants need space to grow properly, bloom, and fruit. As you will also see later when discussing pests and diseases, growing your plants too close together can aid the spread of pests and damage your plants.

In summary, you must maintain control over your indoor plants and consider how they will affect people and pets sharing the same space. Do you have a baby in your home, or are there pets you should be concerned about? How does your indoor garden affect various activities in your home? All of these questions must be answered when setting up your indoor garden.

Chapter 2: What Does It Mean to Be Organic?

There was a time when only hippies and health nuts practiced organic gardening. Today it has become quite commonplace among both indoor and outdoor gardeners. Everyone who wants the best for the environment and wants to feed their family healthy and nutritious food prefers to grow their garden plants organically.

Before discovering chemical fertilizer and pesticides, growing food organically was the natural method used by farmers and gardeners. Hence, the move away from these chemicals to a more holistic and gentler approach is a return to the old norm rather than a new invention.

The organic gardening movement has continued to grow in popularity over the past decade. According to National Gardening Association data, an estimated five-to-twelve million garden products were produced through an all-natural method between 2004 and 2008. By 2019, data from the horticultural experts at Wyevale Garden Centers suggests, more than three-quarters of gardeners avoided using chemicals for their gardens, and up to 46% only use organic fertilizers.

So, what exactly is organic gardening, and how does it differ from the conventional methods of growing garden plants?

What Is Organic Gardening?

There's a short answer and a long answer to this question. Organic gardening simply means gardening without using synthetic products such as artificial fertilizers and chemical pesticides. But that's only an abridged way to explain it. Does this mean you have to leave pests to eat your plants or starve the plants of valuable nutrients just because you don't want to use fertilizers?

A more comprehensive explanation of organic gardening involves the concept of raising plants by replenishing the resources needed to grow them properly, through natural methods. This can be in the form of feeding nutrient-deficient soil with composted plants, using organic fertilizers, or planting legumes that naturally add nitrogen and other nutrients to the soil. It also involves using natural methods to eliminate pests, such as introducing natural enemies of specific insect pests. In essence, organic gardening involves cooperating with nature to grow and care for your plants. You will find that this is helpful to the plants themselves as well as people, wildlife, and the environment at large. The absence of chemical pesticides, for instance, makes an organic garden a safer place for bees to work on pollinating flowers. This is just one of several benefits of natural methods of gardening.

Organic vs. Conventional Gardening

The primary difference between organic and conventional gardening methods is that the former does not use synthetic pesticides and fertilizers. But it is more than merely avoiding artificial chemicals or even swapping them for natural ones.

Organic gardening is a philosophy in itself. It is an approach aimed at supporting the natural environment to achieve the desired results in gardening. In an organically grown garden, the main focus isn't just to see plants grow but to create an ecosystem that provides needed nourishment for the garden plants, insects, and microbes in the soil.

To create this self-sustaining natural ecosystem, efforts must be made toward improving the soil. This is done by mixing in compost to add nutrients and increase the soil's ability to retain water and nutrients. Composts also benefit microbes in the soil that promote the healthy growth of plants.

This natural compost can be made from leaves, grass clippings, kitchen scraps, yard debris, and other organic products commonly available at home. Compost is also available on sale at garden centers or from mulch suppliers. Other aspects of organic gardening include using organic fertilizers to add nutrients to the soil and controlling pests naturally without using chemical products.

Using Organic Fertilizer

Compost adds a bit of nutrients to the soil and increases the soil's ability to hold more nutrients. But composts and organic matter can hardly supply all the nutrients your garden plants require to grow properly and healthily.

You have to make up for the nutrient deficiency somehow, and since chemical fertilizers are not a valid option, organic fertilizers are your next best choice. These are fertilizers produced from natural sources such as natural animal by-products, natural deposits like rock phosphate, and plant products such as seaweed and wood ash.

Organic fertilizers can be produced at home from these natural products or purchased from any gardening supply shop that stocks organic fertilizers. They are characterized by a natural, earthy smell.

Controlling Pests and Diseases without Chemicals

Another aspect of organic gardening is the control of pest and plant diseases using natural methods. Growing your indoor garden crops does not mean you must allow worms, insects, or other pests to infest your garden or produce sick plants.

Since you are trying to avoid using chemicals, you may have to condone some occasional pests in your garden. Rather than a preventive or protective chemical spray, the first line of defense for an organic farmer is vigilance. Inspecting your plants regularly will ensure that pests are detected early, and the problem is fixed as quickly as possible.

Even though there are organic pesticides to eliminate insects and pests, they are not always the first line of defense when a pest problem is detected. An organic gardener will consider other ways to deal with a pest issue before opting for a pesticide.

Most plants are naturally equipped to handle some minor pests and diseases but will be unable to do so effectively if they are stressed, overcrowded, or lack essential nutrients. Some natural ways to handle pest problems include:

- **Interplanting:** Many pests prefer only a specific type of plant. Diversifying your crop base will ensure that you do not lose your entire crop to a single infestation.

- **Introducing Natural Predators:** Many insects and animals prey on other insects while not harming your plants. For instance, an immature ladybug larva is a good example of a beneficial insect, being a natural enemy of many insects and pests. Toads, lizards, and some birds can also help you keep the pest population under control.

- Practicing good sanitation

- Removing infected plants

- Crop rotation

As an organic gardener, you are expected to have a more realistic expectation of keeping pests and diseases at bay. You may not be able to eliminate them from your garden but should be able to keep them below damaging levels through natural means.

In addition to these natural methods, you can also use an organic spray to manage full-blown infestations if they do occur. Examples of products like this include insecticidal soaps, neem oil, and minerals such as sulfur and copper.

Benefits of Gardening the Organic Way

Growing your indoor plants offers plenty of benefits for your plants, you, and the environment. Avoiding the use of chemical products is even more important in an indoor space where whatever spray or chemical you use will be circulated within your space and maybe inhaled by people and pets. Instead of these chemicals, organic gardeners depend on natural biological processes and cultural practices to care for their gardens. Some of the benefits of following this approach include:

Better taste

Fruit and vegetables produced through an organic method are known to have a superior taste. The difference in the flavor of naturally grown food from chemically infused products sold commercially is noticeable to even the dullest palate.

Health

Along with the better taste, this is another reason why organically produced fruit and veggies are more desirable. Chemical sprays for killing pests are released into the air and may settle on surfaces in an indoor garden environment. This can be toxic when inhaled, ingested, or handled by people and pets. An organic garden does not use any chemicals. This means no toxic chemical is entering your body due to any chemical fertilizers, herbicides, and pesticides used on the plants.

In an organic garden, the naturally enriched soil produces all the nutrients the plant needs to grow. This makes it a healthier choice, especially for growing fruit and vegetables for food.

Cost

It is well known that organic produce is typically more costly than conventionally-grown vegetables. But you can eliminate those costs by growing your food organically. This way, you won't have to spend a fortune on organic vegetables from commercial farms or settle for cheaper non-organic produce. You don't have to spend money on buying chemical pesticides and fertilizers either. However, we have to admit that their organic alternatives may be expensive if you opt for them. The good news is that they are used in measured quantity and only when necessary.

Good for the Environment

Organic gardening is beneficial to the environment. Herbicides, chemical pesticides, and synthetic fertilizers have chemical constituents that harm the natural environment. When you use a chemical pesticide, for instance, you also kill off some of the more beneficial insects and upset the balance in nature. Organic gardeners favor the natural process of allowing the soil nutrients to build up naturally and support the increase in the population of beneficial microbes and insects.

It Challenges You to Be More Observant and Involved in the Growing Process

When growing plants organically, you can no longer solve pest issues with brute force or poor soil issues by forcefully adding chemical nutrients. Instead, the process of gardening requires more patient observation to solve these challenges. The goal is to mimic nature as much as possible by nurturing and protecting your garden plants, and this will require you to monitor your plants closely.

Additional Tips for Indoor Organic Gardening

• **Choose Plants That Will Grow Well in Your Indoor Garden:** Different plants require specific conditions to grow properly. Plants that are growing under the right conditions will be healthier, making them less susceptible to pests and diseases. For instance, you should not choose a plant that requires full access to the sun if you don't have a sunny window or have sufficient artificial lighting to provide for this need.

• **Mulching:** This is one of the most useful gardening practices. Not only does it suppress weeds, but mulching can also help conserve water and regulate soil temperature. It also tends to feed your soil organically over time.

• **Diversity Helps:** Planting a mix of crops in your garden will make it difficult for pests and diseases to spread in your garden.

• **Pay Attention to Your Plants:** You can only notice problems easily when you know your plants and pay attention to changes. This helps you to take action before the problem gets out of hand.

Chapter 3: Pests and Fertilizers

One of the major benefits of indoor gardening that seems to draw many to the idea is the allure of not dealing with as many pests as you would have had to deal with in an outdoor garden. Although indoor gardens are indeed less susceptible to pests, this does not mean that you won't have to deal with them at all. But you can rest assured that you will deal with fewer pests (rodents and larger pests are unlikely), and the insect pests you are likely to encounter are typically less difficult to handle.

Indoor garden pest problems occur less frequently than those encountered in an outdoor garden. When they do occur, the insects involved are usually similar. But this does not mean that the response should be the same as that used in an outdoor garden. Indoor pest problems have to be treated differently from those found in a conventional garden.

Best Ways to Prevent Houseplant Pest Infestation

When dealing with indoor pests, outright prevention is the best approach to avoiding an infestation. You can't completely keep insects away from your outdoor garden. However, certain things can be done to reduce the potential of an infestation. These proactive measures will help reduce the chances of an infestation and reduce the population of insect pests to a manageable level should an infestation occur.

Inspection

If you are buying a plant, inspect it first. Check the leaves and stem of the plant before taking it home. And if you do identify any insects, be sure to ask the plant shop owner to have the plant removed, so it does not spread to other plants or get sold to someone else.

Always Use Clean Pots and Soil

The egg and larvae of some insect pests can spread through the re-use of potting and soil. After bringing a new seedling home, ensure that you put it inside a clean or new pot. If you are using an old pot, you should clean the pot with diluted bleach or soapy water. You should use new soil for every new plant you get.

Manually Remove Potential Pests from the Plant and Soil

Sometimes, you may be able to see some insects on the plant or in the soil you intend to plant them in. Insects like sowbugs, millipedes, and pill bugs love the damp and moist environment of garden soil, and while these aren't exactly pests, removing them from the soil is good practice.

Isolate New Plants

Another strategy to help prevent the introduction of pests into your garden is to isolate new plants from the rest of your garden for a few days before introducing them into their new home. During this isolation, you should inspect the leaves and stems of the new plants and only introduce them into your garden if everything checks out fine.

Keep Plants Apart

This approach is not always practical, especially in an indoor garden where you don't have much space to spare, but, if possible, you should grow your plants so that the leaves of the different plants don't touch each other. This is particularly important for new plants. Some insect pests will still be able to spread, but many insects need the leaves in close contact to move from one plant to another. You can curb the spread of such insects by growing the plants further apart.

Types of Pests and How to Deal With Them Naturally

Brown Scales

Scales are common pests of indoor plants that are rather difficult to recognize as a threat; they are quite inconspicuous and don't look like insects at first glance. It will take a closer inspection to identify the brown nubs commonly spotted on the underside of leaves and woody stems as scale.

Brown scales are the most common types of scale. But there are several other varieties. They have a soft brownish body (hence the name) and are oval. Scales typically grow to about 3-4 mm in length.

As their name implies, brown scales have an armored covering and stick closely onto the plant's body, making the stem and leaves to which they are attached appear to have scales on them. While adult scales are primarily immobile, they do a lot of harm to the plant in their immobile state. Their spiky mouthpart allows them to suck away at the sappy juices.

Scales are mobile when they're born. The young scales (also known as crawlers) will disperse along the plant's body or move to nearby plants until they find somewhere they like. They will plant themselves around this spot and will remain there (unless removed) until they reach maturity.

Scales are often a menace to indoor gardens because the optimal temperature of an indoor space favors their growth and reproduction. They can grow and reproduce all year long with no hindrance from the weather.

However, dealing with a scale infestation is relatively easy. Because they are immobile, their spread can be contained to just one plant, which can be removed entirely and discarded. You can also opt to save the plant and meticulously remove the scales.

It is important to note that homemade organic soap sprays don't work on scales, mainly because of their tough outer covering, which acts as a protective shield. So how do you get rid of them?

The trick is to remove the scales from the plant directly, manually. Before you proceed with this, you should place a plastic bag over the plant's soil. This will prevent any scales from falling into the soil from where they remain a threat to the plant.

Next, you can spray the plant with organic rosemary insecticide soap and run your fingers along the leaves and stems of the infected plant to remove the scales. You can use your fingernails or tweezers to pick them out gently. Discard the scales that fall into the plastic bag. Be sure to look the plant over thoroughly.

After removing the scales in this way, hose down the entire plant to get rid of the soap residue. Continue to check the plant over the next few days to confirm there are no more scales.

Mealybugs

Mealybugs have a whitish cottony appearance and are often seen together in clumps on indoor plants. They are not restricted to any particular plant type but can affect almost any houseplants, from succulents to potatoes, pleranda, and Stromanthe, among others.

Dealing with mealybugs is a lot more complex than getting rid of scales. The major reason for this is that, unlike scales, mealybug are quite mobile and will move from one plant to another, especially if the plants are positioned close to each other, quickly spreading all over your indoor garden.

Another factor that makes them difficult to remove is their elusiveness. While their appearance is often an obvious giveaway, mealybugs pick the most elusive places to hide, such as in the crotch or folds of plant leaves. This makes them difficult to spot unless you are particularly observant. They can be challenging to eliminate when you find them, as their cotton-like body produces waxy secretions that protect them from being sprayed by many pesticides.

Finally, mealybugs breed voraciously. Females can lay as many as six hundred eggs in a single pass along the plant's stem or on the underside of a leaf. The eggs hatch quickly (in about a week), and your garden can be infested fast.

This means getting mealybug populations under control as soon as you notice them is quite important. Most people simply discard an infected plant. This works if only one or a few plants have been affected in your garden. You can also spot treat the plant using isopropyl alcohol.

An alternate approach is to introduce a natural enemy of the insect into your garden. Two insects can serve this purpose: the green lacewing and the *Cryptolaemus montrouzieri* (which is often referred to as the "mealybug destroyer," a name that aptly describes its effectiveness for getting rid of mealybug populations).

This approach works better since the insects can easily get into places that you may not be able to reach. You can use both methods (spot treatment and introducing the beneficial insects) to eliminate the pests.

Aphids

Aphids are arguably the most well-known of all houseplant pests. But despite their notoriety, aphids are quite picky regarding the type of garden plants they attack. They are more likely to attack food crops and will never attack tropical house plants.

These insects have piercing mouthparts which they stick into the plant. They feed on the sap of these plants, which is why their appetite is quite specific. In addition to the fact that they drain plants of beneficial sap, they also release a sticky substance that attracts other insects to the plant and provides a medium on which mold can grow. The mold can affect plants and their fruit. This means in addition to dealing with the aphid infestation, you will also have to deal with additional problems the pest brings along with it.

The good thing, however, is that aphids are relatively easy to eliminate. They have a soft body which means you can easily squish them to kill them. If you find aphids on one of your houseplants, you can manually get rid of them. To do this, take the infected plant outside and spray it with a jet of water from a hose. But do this carefully, so the stream of water does not damage the plant. The jet of water should be enough to knock the aphids off the plant without damaging the plant. You can repeat this process every few days until the population of aphids is wholly removed.

Aphid populations can also be controlled by introducing insects that feed on aphids, such as green lacewing larvae or ladybird larvae ("ladybug," in North America).

Common Whitefly

Whiteflies are tiny insects that resemble tiny moths or mealybugs, even though they are more closely related to scales and aphids. Unlike the other insects discussed so far, they are more mobile and can fly off when disturbed. This factor makes them particularly difficult to keep under control.

These pesky insects don't discriminate. They are generalists and will attack pretty much any plant. The fact that they can fly means they can easily spread from one of your garden plants to others.

Adult whiteflies lay eggs that hatch into nymphs in less than a week. The nymphs will crawl to a preferred part of the plant and plant themselves, sucking on the plant sap and growing. After this rest period which typically lasts for three to five weeks, they emerge as adults with tiny white wings.

Both the nymph and adult forms of whiteflies are problematic. They suck the plant sap with their piercing mouthparts which stunts plant growth and causes the leaves to go yellow and eventually fall off. Another problem with whiteflies is that they exude honeydew which attracts mold, weakening the plant in the long run.

The natural methods of controlling whiteflies are similar to those of controlling aphids. You can spray the plant with a burst of water or introduce beneficial insects. In addition to green lace and the ladybird larvae, there is a special whitefly parasite (*Encarsia formosa*) that lays its egg on both the pupae and larval stages of the whitefly, destroying them. Whiteflies, like aphids, are also attracted to the color yellow and can be caught with yellow sticky traps.

Red Spider Mites

Spider mites are not strictly insects, even though they belong to the same broad class (Arthropods). They have singular notoriety among the most common insect pests that attack indoor plants, mainly because they are quite difficult to eliminate.

First, they are so tiny they are nearly invisible to the naked eyes. You may not be able to make out individual mites without a magnifying glass. In most cases, you will only notice signs of their presence, such as a reddish film on the leaves, signs of leaf damage, or reddish-brown spots. This is particularly problematic since visual inspection is the most common way to check for infestations before bringing a new plant into the home.

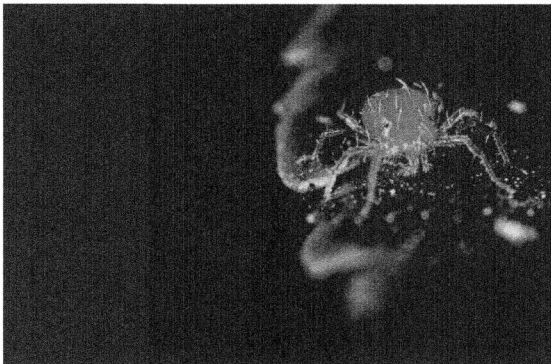

However, if spotted in time, you can quickly implement a measure that helps to control the mite population and eliminate them. You can wash the plant under a stream of water to remove mites. Next, you should modify the humidity level in your indoor garden. Mites thrive under dry conditions, so increasing the humidity level with a humidifier would help eliminate the red mite population. Natural predators like the lacewing larvae, pirate bugs, and some other mites such as *Phytoseiulus sp* can also help eliminate spider mites naturally.

Fungus Gnats

Fungus gnats aren't exactly plant pests in the strictest form. The adult insects do not affect the plants as much as they annoy people. But they are still a problem for indoor gardening since they can make having a garden indoors a frustrating experience.

Fungus gnats are similar in appearance to fruit flies, but they are quite different. They are weak fliers. You are likely to find them circling the soil, especially when you have fresh, damp compost.

While the adult gnat is hardly a problem to indoor gardening, the larvae can feed on plant materials. But they will hardly ever do this. They prefer to feed on fungi in moist soil instead. But if the fungi population is not sufficient, they may eat plants.

Adult gnats are easy to trap. They love to fly around the soil and are attracted to yellow sticky traps. You can also introduce natural predators like the *Stratiolaelaps scimitus* to feed on the gnat.

Thrips

Thrips are not as common as the other insects covered so far in this chapter, but they can also be a problem because they spread rather quickly and are generalists, meaning they can attack pretty much every houseplant.

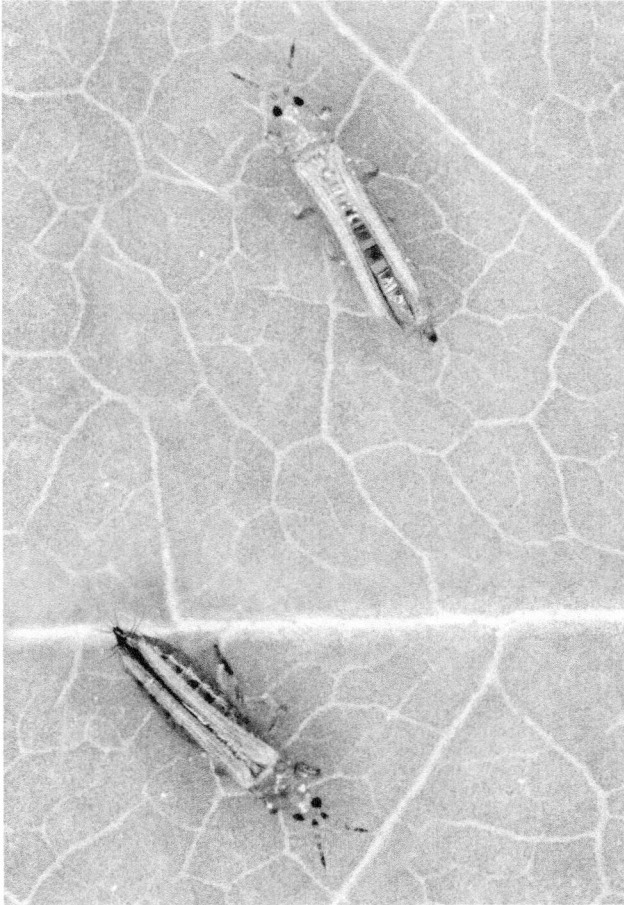

Thrips are also quite destructive. They puncture the outer layer of the plant body, causing discoloration.

Fortunately, thrips have natural predators like the *Neoseiulus cucumeris* and the Minute Pirate Bugs (*Orius insidiosus*), which can help get rid of them. They can also be trapped using blue-colored sticky traps.

Fertilizers

Houseplants show apparent signs when their conditions are not right. They will wilt if they don't get enough water, and their leaves will turn pale when they're not getting enough sunlight. The signs of poor nutrient supply, however, aren't always so obvious, which makes it even trickier to determine when to fertilize or even whether to do it at all. The only sign you will see as the consequence of a lack of needed nutrients is stunted growth, which takes careful observation and familiarity with normal growth rates to notice.

So how do you know when to fertilize your plants, and how often should it be done? Since noting the signs is something of a skill/science/art, most people simply decide to fertilize their indoor garden on a schedule. This approach works great for most indoor gardeners.

Another common problem is that of how to fertilize safely or correctly. In more recent times, the trend has evolved to favor using organic fertilizers rather than conventional chemical fertilizers. I prefer organic fertilizers because they help the soil to create a sustainable environment for the plant, rather than just adding nutrients.

Organic fertilization creates healthy soil, which, in turn, creates healthier plants. Organic fertilization mimics nature in that it relies on fungi and other beneficial microbes in the soil to release nutrients to plants slowly.

These organic supplements encourage the growth of these naturally occurring organisms. Unlike conventional chemical fertilizers that add concentrated forms of nutrients directly to the soil, organic products enable the soil itself to provide nutrients to the plants.

Organic fertilizers often contain humic acids (the totally decomposed remains of organic material) and some desirable microorganisms that produce nutrients like iron and compounds such as polysaccharides, glycoproteins, and hydrophobins. They can be derived from a wide range of organic sources such as animal waste and animal products or by-products, such as blood meal, feather meal, bone meal, kelp, and fish. You can fertilize your soil organically by purchasing certified organic products that are nutrient-rich or make your homemade compost using natural products.

Organic fertilizers may also contain natural products like gypsum, which supplies nutrients like sulfur and calcium and also helps to improve soil structure by loosening compacted soil. This makes it easier for your plant roots to grow as they should.

Healthy Organic Fertilizers Feed Plants

High-quality organic fertilizer products release nutrients through a slow process as they decompose naturally. The nutrients produced are released at a rate that is easy for the plants to digest.

Organic fertilizers are derived from natural sources and provide consistent nourishment over a more extended period rather than just a burst of nutritional supplementation like the chemical products do. The goal is not just to help your plant grow faster or larger for a short while, but to make them healthy and self-sustaining in the long run. This way, instead of depending on you for a repetitive supply of synthetic nutrients, the soil can provide the nutrients the plants need to feed on.

By increasing the organic matter component of your soil, you also enhance the overall structure of the soil. This boosts the ability of your soil to retain water and increases its ability to release nutrients to plants when needed. When done right, organic fertilization can also help suppress certain plant diseases.

Organic Fertilizers Are Safer

Most organic fertilizer products (whether store-bought or made at home) are low in nutrients. For most of these products, their NPK (nitrogen, phosphate, and potassium) ratio, which is typically printed on the product label, is usually less than 10. This low concentration makes organic fertilizers safer for your plant because they're unlikely to burn the roots and leaves of your garden plants like chemical fertilizers often do.

The nutrients contained in organic fertilizers are not used or absorbed directly by the plant. In many cases, the nutrients they contain have to be converted into forms usable by the plant in the soil before being used. The release rate depends on the soil microbes and may even be released even more slowly during cold seasons when the microbes are not very active.

Also, unlike many conventional chemical fertilizers, organic fertilizers don't form a crust on your garden soil. Instead, they further aid the soil structure. This enhances the rate at which water and nutrients move in the soil. Organic fertilizers also provide food for beneficial microbes in the soil that break down nutrients and help prevent plant diseases.

Organic fertilizers are also easier to apply, and you are less likely to destroy your plants with them inadvertently. Inorganic fertilizers often come in concentrated forms, which are easily dissolved in water. This makes them easy to apply, but it also means they are released relatively quickly. There's the risk of applying too much of it, which can burn your plant's roots, so you need to carefully read and adhere to the instructions. Some chemical fertilizers also contain certain salts in potentially harmful amounts and may aid weed seeds' growth.

Organic fertilizers are often more expensive than chemical alternatives. This is the major determining factor that limits their large-scale application. You also need more volume per garden area, since they are not as concentrated as chemical products and will supply fewer nutrients when you compare them pound for pound. But, in the long run, they offer numerous benefits that make them a preferred option for safe and friendly soil fertilization.

Types of Houseplant Fertilizers

Fertilizers for houseplants come in different forms. They can be liquid, granular (or solid), or in the form of slow-release fertilizers. Each fertilizer type has its unique qualities, which determine how they are applied, how often they should be used, and how they affect your houseplants.

Liquid Houseplant Fertilizer

Liquid fertilizers are just as the name suggests. They are in liquid form and have to be mixed to the right strength before application. Liquid fertilizers are usually not as strong as granular types, so they often need to be applied more frequently. There are both organic and inorganic liquid fertilizers.

Organic liquid fertilizers are often made from plant and animal material but may also contain natural mineral products. Ingredients used for making organic liquid fertilizer include compost tea, fish emulsion, liquid kelp, liquid bone meal, plant extracts, humic acid, and rock phosphates.

Since liquid fertilizers are not as strong as granular fertilizers, they are unlikely to burn your plant's roots. In addition to adding nutrients to the soil, organic liquid fertilizers also enhance the growth of your garden plants because they contain an abundance of micronutrients, vitamins, plant hormones, and trace elements that make plants healthier and stronger.

Granular Houseplant Fertilizer

Granular fertilizers come either as compressed fertilizer spikes or in loose pellet form. The pelletized forms are sprinkled on the soil surface while the spikes are pushed into the soil.

Granular fertilizers can be made from both chemical and organic ingredients. Organic products can be made from animal and plant-based ingredients as well as some natural minerals. Common ingredients include bone meal, worm castings, limestone, rock phosphate, and sulfate of potash.

You should be able to tell if a granular fertilizer is made from organic or inorganic ingredients by checking the ingredients list.

Slow-Release Houseplant Fertilizers

Slow-release fertilizers are typically synthetic fertilizers designed to work very slowly. Also commonly referred to as time-release fertilizer, this fertilizer has liquid nutrients wrapped in a coating that gradually breaks down over time. This releases the nutrients in small doses over a longer period.

The main benefit of slow-release products is that you don't have to fertilize your garden as often as with the other two types of fertilizers. Slow-release organic fertilizers are less common and tend to be more expensive initially.

What to Consider When Choosing Organic Fertilizer

Organic fertilizers are great, but there are different types, and they are not all created equal. To choose the best one for your indoor garden, you should consider how fast they act as well as other aspects of ease and convenience. Different crops have different nutritional requirements, all of which you have to consider when choosing your preferred fertilizer.

Dry vs. Liquid

Dry organic fertilizers need to be worked into the soil for maximum results. Unlike chemical products that dissolve when water is added, dry organic fertilizers are not water-soluble. Rather, they are broken down by microbes in the soil and the nutrients released are gradually absorbed by the roots of the plants. This means they provide slow feeding for the plants over a longer period compared to the liquid alternative.

On the other hand, liquid organic fertilizers are recommended if you prefer a solution that releases nutrients quickly to your plants. They come in a concentrated form that is diluted with water to the appropriate strength. Generally, liquid fertilizers are the preferable option if you're looking to give your plant a strategic nutrient boost during the appropriate season.

Nutrients

Another factor to consider is the nutritional composition of your fertilizer. Typically, most fertilizers contain significant percentages of nitrogen, phosphorus, and potassium. These are typically indicated with the letters N-P-K on the product packaging, with a numerical indication of the percentage of each nutrient. Thus, your choice of fertilizer product to use should consider the beneficial component it contains and the effect it will have on your plant.

> • **Nitrogen:** Nitrogen is an abundant element in chlorophyll which gives plants their lush green color and helps food production. An abundance of these nutrients promotes leafy growth.

> • **Phosphorus:** This element is essential for many of the major functions of a plant, including flowering, fruiting, and root development.

• **Potassium:** Potassium is necessary to regulate many of a plant's metabolic processes. This means it is important for plant growth and boosts the plant's ability to defend itself against diseases and pests.

Organic fertilizers may also be formulated to contain different micronutrients, including boron, zinc, manganese, copper, iron, chlorine, and molybdenum. Although they're usually included in only small quantities, a small dose of these micronutrients can contribute to the overall health and growth of the plant. You should check on the packaging for the micronutrient composition of any fertilizer product you intend to buy.

In addition to these nutrients, organic fertilizers may also include some dormant fungi and bacteria cultures that become active in the soil and help to unlock and release nutrients. Many of these microbes already exist naturally in healthy soil. Still, their population may be sparse in indoor garden soils, which is why supplementing them through your fertilizer supply is a great idea.

Plant Type

Different plants have varying nutritional needs. This will affect the type of fertilizer to use and how often it will be applied. Fertilizers often have varying nutrient ratios printed on the label because some plants need specific nutrients more than others. You will probably spot the figures written as "5-10-10", "0-5-0", "5-10-5", and so on, indicating the N-P-K composition of the fertilizer. Consider this when fertilizing your garden:

Leafy plants like salad greens need a lot of nitrogen. Hence, you should use fertilizers with high nitrogen content.

Fruiting plants such as cucumbers, tomatoes, and corn need a more balanced ratio of the different NPK nutrients, all at high levels.

Trees and shrubs have low nutritional requirements. This means fertilizer application should be made less frequently, and moderately.

Consider the Desired Effect

Perhaps the most important factor to consider when shopping for organic fertilizer is the ultimate goal you have in mind. For instance, if long-term soil fertility is your intention, you are better off using slow-feeding granular fertilizer instead of liquid fertilizer, which is better suited for when you want to give your plant a burst of nutrients.

Some fertilizer types also serve the dual purpose of building your soil and supplying nutrients. Examples of these are worm castings and compost. These types are best considered if you intend to boost the soil structure of your garden. They also add to the microbial population of your soil. But they may not do much in terms of adding nutrients. Some fertilizer types, such as mulch, also serve the purpose of soil amendment. Keep all of these uses in mind when determining your preferred fertilizer type.

Consider the Soil Condition

Unless you pick a fertilizer that boosts soil structure, most organic fertilizers don't improve the soil structure at all. If this is a major consideration for you, you should look for fertilizers with a generous organic matter composition. You can also prepare your organic matter compost using leaf mold, hardwood chips, and aged manure. This can then be followed up with regular fertilizers.

For the best assurance, you should test your soil first to determine its composition. This will include checking for the current nutrient level, organic content, and pH (acidity or alkalinity). Knowing this will help you to establish a standard fertilization regime that gives your garden plants just what they need.

How to Fertilize Plants Based on Type and Season

Every houseplant is unique and has specific nutrient requirements. This is why the process, frequency, and quantity of fertilizer used on them tend to differ. That's not to say you have to be aware of the different fertilization processes of every garden plant.

You should, by all means, get familiar with the specific needs and general care of the plants you intend to raise. But most of the most common houseplants have closely similar requirements. This means you may not need to treat each of them separately. A unified approach optimized for all your garden plants should be good enough for all of them.

While some houseplants don't need as much fertilizer as others, and others need to be fertilized more frequently, it is possible to develop a fertilizer plan that satisfies both the heavy feeders and those that only need low amounts of fertilizer.

The environmental and soil conditions vary with each season of the year, even in an indoor garden. The temperature and humidity levels are never consistent all year round. Additionally, fertilization needs tend to vary by season. Since these conditions affect houseplants just as it affects outdoor plants, you must pay attention and follow a plan that considers these different nutritional needs across different seasons.

Spring Houseplant Fertilizer Schedule

The active growing season of most plants is in the spring. But fertilization can begin before the start of the season. Generally, it is recommended that you start fertilizing your indoor garden about eight weeks before the expected date of the last spring frost. This means fertilization should typically start around the time when the days start to lengthen. During this time, your houseplant should be in a semi-dormant state, gearing up for a period of active growth.

But this pre-growth season fertilization should not be done at full strength. Instead, the first three applications should be at about half of the stipulated strength for the fertilizer you are using. This means using half the recommended amount for a granular product or mixing the fertilizer to half strength for liquid fertilizer.

Summer Houseplant Fertilization Schedule

Summer is typically a period of active growth for most houseplants. The light levels are always the highest during this period regardless of which part of your home they're placed in, which means they will have higher nutrient requirements during this season to achieve the best growth profile possible.

As the summer season begins, you should switch to a full fertilization regimen for your houseplants. The amount of fertilizer to be used and how frequently it should be applied depends on the specific type of fertilizer you are using. It is usually a monthly or bi-weekly period for liquid fertilizers. Granular products, on the other hand, are applied less frequently. There are also slow-release fertilizers that take more time to release their nutrients. For these products, you only need a single application every three or four months.

Fall & Winter Houseplant Fertilization Schedule

You should begin to reduce the frequency of fertilization and the amount you use as you go into the fall season. This switch can start before the first expected fall frost for the season. But don't cut fertilizer application abruptly. You can cut down the application to about half the regular quantity then gradually stretch out the frequency of application as you get nearer to winter.

For obvious reasons, there is no need to fertilize your houseplants during winter. This is not a period of active growth for most houseplants, so there is no need to fertilize them. You risk burning the roots of your plant if you do.

However, there are some specific situations where this rule does not apply. Suppose you live in a climate where things don't get frozen up during winter, and you still manage to get some sunlight. Then, in that case, it's okay to continue fertilizer application (preferably at half the regular strength and at a reduced frequency). Also, those living in a tropical climate where the weather stays warm all year round can keep fertilizing their houseplant on a regular schedule throughout the year.

Chapter 4: Creating Indoor Sunlight

The difference in light conditions is one of the biggest distinctions between gardening indoors and outdoors. The fact remains that the darkest shade outdoors still gets more sunlight than the sunniest window spot indoors.

Even if your plant is planted in the shade outdoors, there is still sufficient light bouncing at it from different angles, providing a 360-degree supply of sunlight to the plant. Indoor plants often only get light from one source, which is the sunny window in the room. This phenomenon is referred to as an exponential reduction in photon exposure.

Why Sunlight Is Crucial for Plants

Like all living things, plants need food to stay alive and grow. The only difference, of course, is that plants don't eat directly as animals do. Instead, they synthesize their food, and an essential ingredient for this is light. Plants rely on photosynthesis, which uses light captured by their chloroplast to create sugars needed for growth and sustenance. Without sufficient light (in terms of both quality and quantity), plants cannot produce their food.

The quality of light refers to the type (color) of the light. Light energy comes in different wavelengths, each with a specific color. Plants see lights differently from how humans and animals see light. The spectrum of light that we see and/or consider helpful differs from what a plant needs. Green light, for instance, is useless to plants since they reflect most of it. Instead, they absorb light of other colors which is useful to them. Plants can also use light in the invisible spectrum, such as ultraviolet light and some infrared lights.

We also have to consider the impact of light on plants in terms of the quantity of light. This refers to the brightness or intensity of light that the plant can get in its current position. Generally, the more light photons the leaves of a plant can get, the more energy it can produce to grow faster. While other ingredients like the water and carbon monoxide composition of the air are important, the plants will only produce the sugars and nutrients they need when they get light of the right color and intensity. This is why some plants will not produce fruit or flowers if the right lighting conditions are not met.

Different Types of Light

When planning an indoor gardening project, one of the most important things to analyze is the light conditions in your space and how this will affect the plants you will be bringing into your garden. In gardening, light conditions can be classified as high, medium, or low-light. Each of these light conditions is best suited to specific plant species. You must identify the light condition in your space and compare it to the light requirements of the plants you intend to add to your indoor garden.

High-Light

Also known as full sun or bright light, this sunlight condition refers to a situation where there is no barrier between a plant and the light source. The high-light area of your garden is the part of the room where the plant will get direct access to the sun. Brightly lit parts of a room typically stem from windows being on the southern-exposure walls in the northern latitudes and the northern-exposure walls in the southern latitudes.

Generally, high-light plants such as succulents, Monstera, and ficus should be placed in the brightest spot in your garden room. They should be positioned as close to the window as possible and never more than two or three feet away from it).

High-light areas tend to be warmer than the rest of the room. This means your plants are more likely to dry out faster here than in other parts of the room. Plants positioned here should be checked frequently and replenished with water quite often.

Most plants that are grown for their flowers usually grow better in high-light conditions. Other examples of high-light plants include cacti, citrus plants, hibiscus, and some herbs such as lavender, thyme, and basil.

Medium-Light

This refers to filtered light or light that has been diffused. When there is a sheer object, such as a curtain, or a partial obstruction, such as the end of a bookcase, between the light source and a placement position, the light at that point is referred to as filtered or dappled light.

Some plants are particularly adapted to thrive in this condition. Such plants, whose natural habitat is the forest floor where they are usually shaded by the sun, cannot handle the harsh rays of direct light and will survive better in medium-light conditions.

Medium-light plants will grow well indoors in well-lit areas such as east-facing or west-facing window spots since they only receive a high dose of light during morning or afternoon hours but should nonetheless be positioned away from direct sunlight. Plants in medium-light areas are not likely to dry out as quickly as those in high-light areas, and hence will require less watering

Ferns and aroid plants are good examples of medium-light plants. Other examples include Amaryllis, elephant ears, Norfolk Island pine, and rubber plants.

Low-Light

Low-light areas of your garden room refer to areas that get no direct sunlight. This area is either too far away from the light source, or the light source is significantly obstructed. A low-light area means there is a lesser energy source which means less food for the plant. But some plants survive well in these conditions.

Low-light conditions do not mean a complete absence of light. It can be described as a light that is bright enough to read a book if your eyes are good. The northern windows of your garden room, if you live in the far northern latitudes, are a good example of a low-light area. The condition here is similar to the condition of understory environments on forest floors where the sunlight is entirely obstructed by the branches of larger plants growing overhead. In these low-light environments, plants grow more slowly. But they also require less water, so you should avoid overwatering them.

Without supplementary light, a low-lighting condition is usually not conducive to starting seeds. But certain plants will still survive in this condition. Examples of low-light plants include Chinese evergreen, cast-iron plants, Ponytail palm, and Dumb cane.

Types of Artificial Light for Indoor Growing

Sunlight offers the full spectrum of light wavelengths needed by plants to produce food and thrive. But indoor spaces hardly ever get sufficient light, both in terms of quality and quantity. The implication of this is that even in high-light areas of your home, you may still need supplementary lighting.

Artificial light also makes it possible to grow plants under a wide range of lighting conditions, including indoor gardens in spaces where natural lighting is limited, such as windowless rooms. While some plants will grow in low-light conditions, they may never bloom if they don't get sufficient light. Using artificial light is the only way to get them to bloom and fruit at the right time. Different types of artificial lights supply lights of different wavelengths (colors).

Fluorescent

Fluorescent lights were known for being the most economical artificial lighting choice before the LED breakthroughs. Nowadays, they can be found in both the old-style double-pin ends and in the form of compact (CFL) bulbs or tubes that can be screwed into regular lamp sockets. The tube-like bulbs come in varying size ranges labeled T5, T8, and T12. Narrower fluorescent tubes are typically brighter and more efficient because of their smaller surface area.

One of the major advantages of fluorescent lamps is that they don't get as hot as many other lighting options. Additionally, fluorescent bulbs make use of 75% less energy than comparable incandescent lamps. Thus, you only need a 25-watt fluorescent lamp to produce as much light as a 100-watt incandescent bulb.

Kelvin is a basic unit of color temperature used to measure the whiteness of a light's output; it's the degree of visual warmth or coolness of a light source. The higher the degree of Kelvin, the bluer, or "cooler," the lamp appears; the lower the degree of Kelvin, the redder, or "warmer," it appears.

Fluorescent light bulbs can be generic or a full spectrum of light. Generic fluorescent tubes have a higher coefficient of blue light. Blue light is known to aid foliage growth. Full-spectrum fluorescent lights, on the other hand, contain a mix of colors. They can either be cool or warm. As a general rule of thumb, cool white light is more recommended because white light tends to contain a full spectrum of light with various wavelengths. Fluorescent lights are best positioned about a foot away from the leaves of your plant. Fluorescent lights are most ideal for low-to-medium-light houseplants. They are also good for starting vegetable gardens.

Incandescent

Incandescent lights are ideal for growing low-light houseplants like vines, ferns, or dracaenas but have limited applications for growing higher-light plants. This is mainly because they give off most of their energy as heat rather than light. Only 10% of the energy produced by an incandescent bulb is released as light. The remaining 90% is given off as heat.

Because incandescent lights give off a lot of heat, they should be positioned far enough away from your plant not to cook it. This is why they should not be used for light-loving plants like cacti, succulents, and tropicals.

A more practical application of incandescent light bulbs is to supplement and balance out the blue light produced by generic fluorescent lights. To mix these two lights, you should use one-third of incandescent light with two-thirds of fluorescent in terms of wattage. The light produced by incandescent lamps is in the red wavelength. This is especially useful if you are trying to get your garden plants to bloom.

LED

LED stands for light-emitting diode. Nowadays, this is the most common type of grow light for an indoor garden. LED bulbs are known for their high energy efficiency. Like fluorescent light, they produce less heat and very bright light.

Thanks to the diversity of **LED** technology, **LED** light is highly customizable. There are different varieties, including stand-alone clip-on, screw-in bulbs, desktop lights, and so on. There are also some high-intensity varieties suited for use in greenhouses.

LEDs can be customized to produce both blue and red light that plants need for growth and fruiting. Horticulture LEDs, the most popular variety of this type of light, are designed to produce light at the wavelengths that plants need the most. These are better options compared to general-use LEDs. You may also find some varieties of

LEDs that have been programmed to emit light at different intensities for different times of the day or synchronized with mobile phones for remote control of light levels.

How Plants Are Affected by Too Little or Too Much Light

Plants use light for photosynthesis. This process produces the energy and materials that plants need to thrive. The glucose produced during photosynthesis forms the leaves, stems, flowers, and other plant parts. Because sunlight is so important to plants, a lack of it can adversely affect plants in various ways.

Changes in Leaf Color

Naturally, most plants have leaves with a dark green color attributable to the chlorophyll content of the cells in the leaves. This chlorophyll is what the plant uses to absorb incoming light for photosynthesis. But when the chlorophyll in the leaves doesn't work optimally due to poor light exposure, the plant will gradually lose its leaf color and become paler, until the leaves eventually turn yellow and fall off.

Plant Growth

Another obvious effect of poor light conditions is stunted growth. This is not always noticeable, especially if the plant has remained in a low-light position throughout its growth period. But you will most likely notice the change if you have recently changed the plan's position from a sunny window to a darker part of your garden room. Some plant seeds will not even grow under low light conditions until they are exposed to the right kind of light.

Extended Internodes and Leaf Size

Some parts of the plant will naturally modify to adapt to the insufficient light supply. If the light supply is enough for the plant to grow slowly but is still insufficient to meet its needs, you may notice that the size of the leaves will reduce, and the space between them (called the internode) will grow. These signs indicate that your plant is not getting the optimal amount of sunlight that it needs.

Leaning

Plants can respond to light and will normally grow in the direction of the light supply. Due to this tendency, called "phototropism," the stem and leaves of certain garden plants may grow leaning towards the natural light supply to ensure that they get the maximum amount of sunlight possible under less-than-optimal light conditions. Using artificial light such as a fluorescent tube or simply turning the plant towards the light source regularly are two simple solutions that work for this problem.

What Happens When Plants Are Exposed to Too Much Light?

When discussing the effects of excessive light on plants, we can look at it in terms of two major factors: the intensity or brightness of the light and the duration of the light per day. Duration in this sense refers to the number of hours of light that the plant gets daily. Intensity, on the other hand, is related to the quantity of light it gets. These two factors affect the growth and health of plants differently, but light intensity is the more important of these two because it has a more direct effect on plant growth and performance.

How Excessive Light Duration Affects Plants

The major impact of the long duration of light on a plant is on its growth and fruiting cycle. Generally, plants will continue to grow normally and healthily even when exposed to light indefinitely, as long as the intensity of the light is not excessive. Plants grow faster in the dark because most of their essential metabolic processes occur in the dark. Therefore, some plants will not be able to enter some of their most important growth phases or bloom at the right time if the darkness-and-light cycles are disrupted. This is a phenomenon referred to as "photoperiodism."

The impact of a long light duration like this varies from one plant to the other. For plants like Christmas Cacti, Kalanchoe, and others like them (also known as short-day plants) that need extended periods in the darkness to bloom, this extended light duration implies that they will not be able to grow properly or flower at the right time. The opposite is the case when you're dealing with long-day plants.

How Excessive Light Intensity Affects Plants

While excessive light duration does not directly harm plants, real problems occur when the supply of light is too intensive. This is mostly because excess light (high-intensity light) is often converted to heat energy. Like all living organisms, plants will attempt to attain a balanced temperature by dissipating excess heat energy, usually by using up some of its water in an attempt to cool off.

This will have a cyclic effect on vital processes such as photosynthesis that require the presence of water. Additionally, if the high-intensity light persists and the rate of heat production exceeds the capacity of the plant to dissipate heat, the plant will eventually suffer heat damage, showing signs such as browning and yellowing of the leaves, crispy or curled edges, and dropping leaves.

Furthermore, the high light intensity will cause the soil to dry out faster than normal, making it impossible for the plant to draw moisture from it. This further accelerates the rate of dehydration, leading to a wide range of damage. How much damage occurs and how soon it does depends on the tolerance level of the plant in question.

What to Look for in Growing Light

If you are buying artificial grow-lights for the first time, navigating the process of picking the right one for your garden plants is not going to be a simple task. It's not just about picking the right type of grow-light. Different products come in a variety of qualities and wattages and are made by various manufacturers. You also have to consider factors relating to your plants themselves, such as the type of plant and how much space you have. These factors can make it challenging to find the perfect grow- light that will suit the unique needs of your garden plants. But with some research, you should be able to crack the code and find just the right product for you. Here are some of the most important things to consider in choosing grow-lights.

Determine the Plants You Are Growing

To a large extent, the type of artificial light to buy depends on what you intend to use them for. You need to know the kind of light that the plant you will be growing will need. After you determine the type of plants you will be growing in your indoor garden, you can do some research to determine the conditions they thrive best in and the type of lights that will help achieve those conditions. For instance, while blue lights are great for merely growing plants, you will need red lights if your plants need to bloom and fruit.

Light Intensity

This refers to the brightness of the light. There is often a problem here because light intensity can be measured in different ways. Therefore, the packaging label on two different bulbs can indicate their light intensity in different ways using completely different metrics. It makes comparing their output quite tricky to do.

Some of the most common units of measurements you may encounter include:

- **PPF:** The Photosynthetic Photon Flux refers to how much plant-usable light a light bulb can release per second. The unit of PPF is $\mu mol/m^2 * s$ (micromoles of light per square meter times seconds), or in simpler terms, the number of light photons striking a given area over time. A similar unit of measurement to this is the Photosynthetic Photon Flux Density (PPFD) which refers to the amount of usable light that reaches the leaf surface. The PPFD tends to decrease the further away your plant is from the light source.

• **Foot-Candle:** Refers to how much light the plant receives per square foot of its surface area when it is one foot away from the light source. These days this unit is rarely used, but it used to be common in the past.

• **Lumens:** This unit is commonly used to measure the brightness of light bulbs in general but does not directly apply to grow-lights. It measures the brightness of a light source as seen by the human eye rather than the wavelength of light needed by the plant.

• **Watts:** Watts are not units for measuring brightness so much as describing the lamp's energy requirements to produce light. The higher the efficiency of the lightbulb, the fewer watts of energy it will need to produce light. Typically, grow-lights manufacturers indicate the wattage of the lamp along with another measure of light intensity (usually PPF).

Distance from the Light Source

It is particularly important to consider the distance of your light source from your plants when using a light bulb that produces a lot of heat, such as incandescent light or high-pressure sodium lights. But even with more efficient light sources like LEDs and fluorescent lights, you still need to maintain a proper distance for optimal growth and health. How close or far away your light should be placed from your plant also depends on the plant.

• For Seedlings, you should keep the light between 4-6 inches from the plant. But this distance should be adjusted regularly as the plants grow.

• Herbs and hydroponic lettuce: between 6-12 inches

• Flowering houseplants: between 6-12 inches

• Foliage houseplants: between 12-24 inches

This recommendation is for LED and fluorescent lights. The spacing recommendation will be entirely different for incandescent lights and other sources that tend to heat up a lot. Some sources recommend that Incandescent bulbs should be placed at least 24 inches away from your plants.

Light Quality

The light quality refers to the color (or wavelength) of light produced by the lamp. Sunlight produces a spectrum of light that includes light of all wavelengths colored red, orange, yellow, green, blue, indigo, and violet. The part of this spectrum that plants can make use of directly is known as the Photosynthetically Active Radiation (PAR), which is composed mainly of red and blue light. Artificial grow-light technology has evolved to produce light that emits blue and red wavelengths alone or a mixture of these two known as white or balanced light. The exact type of light the grow-light emits will be indicated on the label.

- **Blue Light:** These are most suitable for starting seeds or growing leafy greens and non-flowering plants.

- **Red Light:** This promotes bud formation, which makes it the ideal choice for flowering plants. Red light is also good if you prefer to keep your plants short.

- **White Light:** Also called mixed or balanced light, these bulbs are suitable for all types of plants and at all stages of growth.

Light Duration (Photoperiod)

This refers to how long your plants need to be exposed to light within every 24-hour period. Based on the number of hours of light they need, plants are grouped into three broad categories: short day, day-neutral, and long day.

- **Long-Day Plants:** Examples of long-day plants include African Violets, tuberous begonias, and gloxinia. These plants need more daylight hours than dark hours to bloom.

• **Day-Neutral Plants** are not very sensitive to the length of day or night and will flower regardless of the light conditions they are subjected to (within reason). Examples of plants like this include Abutilon (flowering maple), gerbera daisies, and Crossandra.

• **Short-Day Plants** like Christmas Cacti, poinsettia, and Thanksgiving Cacti need more darkness than light to flower.

Chapter 5: Humidity and Temperature

There are four basic things that plants need for survival: sunlight, nutrients, the right temperature, and moisture. The absence or excess of any of these will upset the balance of your garden plants and lead to poor development. In extreme cases, you may end up losing your plants if any of these factors are not within acceptable levels.

Proper Temperature

The temperature of a space depends on the transfer of heat between the sun and the surrounding air. Since the ambient climate conditions of a place determine the type of plant that can grow there, maintaining the proper temperature is essential for your indoor garden plants. The temperature is constantly changing in the natural environment. But the good thing about indoor gardening is that you can monitor and control the temperature using a wide range of measures, including insulation and installing heating and cooling systems.

Light

In the outdoor environment, plants get all the light they need from sunlight. But they can grow in an indoor space without sufficient sunlight by using artificial light of the right wavelength. Light energy is needed by plants to produce glucose, which is their energy source. They have chloroplast in their leaf cells which contains chlorophyll, a chemical pigment that can absorb light energy used for photosynthesis.

If the plants' cells are not exposed to sufficient light, the growth rate will be slowed down. But light that is too intense can be bad for plants as well. It will heat the plant and the soil it grows in, causing them to dry out. Plants have varying requirements as far as lighting is concerned. While some plants will do well in bright or direct light, others prefer dimmer light.

Water

Along with carbon dioxide, water is an essential ingredient needed by plants for photosynthesis. Without it in sufficient amounts, plants will not be able to produce sufficient food. Water is absorbed by cells in the roots of the plants and is transported to the chloroplasts within the leaves, where photosynthesis takes place.

In addition to its role in photosynthesis, water also helps transport nutrients from the soil to the different parts of the plant. A lack of water will cause the plant to droop, wilt, and die off. Excess water can cause the roots to rot.

Nutrients

Although plants produce their food using water, carbon dioxide, and sunlight, they need additional nutrients to maintain growth. There are at least seventeen different nutrients that plants need to grow and develop properly. These nutrients are obtained via the plant's roots from the soil or growing medium in which the plant grows.

Plant nutrients are grouped into two broad groups. Macronutrients refer to those nutrients needed by the plant in large quantities (mainly nitrogen, potassium, and phosphorus). Nitrogen promotes healthy foliage, and phosphorus is needed for fruiting and flower development, while potassium aids growth and metabolism. Micronutrients, on the other hand, are needed in minute quantities.

The soil in which garden plants grow often contains organic matter and mineral matter which supplies the nutrients needed for survival. Other factors such as the texture of the soil, particle size, and so on determine how many nutrients the soil can retain. Fertilizers (both organic and inorganic) can be introduced to add more nutrients to the soil and boost the overall structure of the soil to increase nutrient retention.

We have discussed how light and nutrients affect plants and supplement them in an indoor garden in the previous chapters. So, this chapter will focus less on these two and more on temperature and moisture balance.

The temperature and humidity balance of an indoor garden is somewhat connected. Any excess or deficiency of one will affect the other. When the temperature is too high, the moisture level will drop, and the plant will dry up faster. Excessive humidity levels can also increase the temperature. Different houseplants have unique needs as far as temperature and moisture go, and you must pay attention to these factors and know how to monitor them for optimal performance, growth, and health of your indoor plants.

Temperature

Maintaining the right temperature is just as important for your indoor plants as it is in an outdoor garden. You cannot grow cool weather plants successfully when the weather is scalding hot or grow heat-loving plants in the cool winter months.

To grow well, most plants need a warm temperature. For heat-loving summer plants such as cucumbers and tomatoes, you need to keep the temperature at about 26° C (79° F) during the daytime and at about 17° C (63° F) during the night.

If your garden room is cooler than this temperature, you have to figure out a way to raise the temperature or simply stick to winter crops that are happy with a temperature of 10° C (50° F)-to-21° C (70° F) during the day and 7° C (45° F)-to-12° C (54° F) at night. Your plants will grow better if you keep them as close to the optimal growing temperature as possible.

Low temperature doesn't exactly damage plants. Rather, the plants will go into a period of dormancy when the temperature drops too low and start growing again as the days warm up. They may also get diseases and may be unable to recover if the temperature isn't right.

Temperature for an Indoor Edibles Window-Garden

If you plan to grow your garden plants in a heated room, you don't have to overthink the effect of temperature on your plants. In this case, you can simply select indoor plants suited to grow best at the average temperature of the room. For instance, if you're growing plants in a cool basement, then plants like parsley would be great. But if you are growing in a warm kitchen, then plants like basil would be a better option.

If the grow-room is not heated, you will need to provide supplementary heating during the cold months. Cool-weather plants like cabbage, greens, and some herbs are not affected by the winter chill. It is the hot-weather plants that you should be more worried about.

Windows do a lot to warm up your grow-room. Generally, the more windows your house has, the warmer the garden room will be when the day is sunny. But you may also need additional heating for night times, overcast days, or if you live in a region that does not get a lot of heat from sunlight.

Monitoring the Temperature of a Grow-Room

If you are serious about growing plants indoors, you must have an idea of the indoor temperature in your space. In the first place, this will determine the type of indoor plants you can grow. It will also help you know if your room needs to be modified for the kind of plant you intend to grow.

It is also recommended that you install a thermometer in your grow room to monitor the temperature continuously. You cannot assume the temperature in the growing area will remain the same all the time, since indoor temperatures may vary widely in response to the outdoor temperature.

You may also have to invest in measures to insulate your growing space to keep it from getting too cold or freezing up during the cold winter months. This is particularly important if your grow-room has a lot of windows.

Extremely high temperatures may also be a problem on hot summer days, especially when growing plants close to a sunny window or an area that gets direct sunlight. Be sure to check the temperature on days like this to make the right decisions about cooling the space or moving the plant out of direct sunlight.

Soil Temperature for an Indoor Garden

When most people think about the temperature in an indoor garden, they only think about the room temperature and seldom talk about the soil temperature. This is mainly because indoor gardens grow plants in containers, so the soil temperature is usually in line with the room temperature.

But extremely cold or hot temperatures can also affect the soil in your containers, affecting the roots of your plant. If the temperature of the room is too cool or the floor where your plants sit is too cold, the soil may get too cold as well, and this will make it difficult for the plant to absorb nutrients. You may place a Styrofoam barrier or any other form of insulation material between the container and the floor. A heat mat can also help to keep the plant warm when the room is freezing.

Even if you grow your plant hydroponically (without soil), you still need to pay attention to the temperature. You can use a water heater to keep the water from freezing up in the cold. In the summer months, you should insulate the plant container and use a brightly colored container that reflects heat effectively.

Water

Water is crucial to all life but essential for plants because they use it during photosynthesis for food production. Even hardy plants in the desert need some quantity of water.

In addition to its role in photosynthesis, the sugar produced in the leaves is transported throughout the plant by water. It also helps the transportation of additional nutrients from the soil through the roots of the plants to all the other parts where they are needed. Water also helps plant cells to maintain their turgidity. If a plant does not have sufficient water in its cells, it will shrivel, and the plant will begin to droop. So not only is a plant malnourished when it does not get a sufficient supply of water, but it is also weak and will be unable to support its own weight.

Water plays an important role in temperature control for plants. As water evaporates from the plant surface, cooler water is drawn up from the roots to replace the lost water. This cools the plant as the water circulates through it.

Of course, different plants have different water requirements. Water-loving plants will be more affected by a lack of water than plants that have evolved to survive for a long time under drought conditions.

In the outdoor environment, it is difficult to limit the amount of water your plants get. If you live in an area that gets a lot of rain, you can only take precautions like ensuring that the plant's soil is properly drained.

This is hardly a problem in an indoor garden since the volume of water your plant gets is completely under your control. All you have to do is ensure that you know how often your plant should be watered and follow through with this, bearing in mind that other factors like temperature and humidity affect how your plant absorbs water. For instance, a plant positioned close to a source of light near a window may need to be watered more often than the same plant in a low-light area since the rate of evaporation is higher near the window.

Plants absorb water through their root systems. The water is then transported up the plant through the stem to the plant's leaves, flowers, and fruit. Water in plants is transported through a capillary-like network of vessels known as xylem vessels.

Knowing the function of water and the effects of excess or insufficient water on plant growth will help you understand why you need to water your garden plants appropriately for their health and growth. Even in an indoor garden, watering can be just enough, too little, or too much. If the plant's roots get too much water that they cannot absorb, they will begin to rot. The plant will also be unable to absorb enough oxygen, and other nutrients from the soil since the process of absorption depends on concentration differentials between the plant roots and the surrounding soil. The plant will be unable to grow healthily if the root is damaged.

In maintaining water balance, there are a few things to keep in mind:

- Different plants have different water needs
- Temperature and other external factors can affect how often you need to water your plants. Hence, the

standard minimum or maximum water requirements for your plants may vary based on these and other factors.

- You can easily check by inspecting your garden soil. Generally, if you stick your finger in the soil and it feels moist, it has enough water. But if it feels dry, you need to add some water to it.

- Signs of dehydration include an abnormally light pot and soil pulling away from the sides of the container. In these cases, you should water the plants.

Humidity in an Indoor Garden

When considering how much moisture a plant gets, you have to think not just about how much water is in the soil but also the amount of moisture in the air.

The temperature and humidity of a room are connected. The effect of humidity in an indoor garden space is two-directional. Plants release moisture into the air, which means you are likely to notice a substantial increase in the humidity level in your indoor space when you begin to grow plants indoors. At the same time, excessive or extremely low humidity levels can adversely affect plants as well.

How to Reduce Humidity Levels in Your Grow Space

High humidity can make your home feel uncomfortable. Rooms feel hotter than they are when there is too much moisture in the air. Excess moisture can also affect plants negatively. The following are some of the ways to keep the humidity level under control in your indoor garden:

- **Raise the Temperature:** Temperature and humidity are intricately connected. If you start noticing a buildup of moisture in your space, you can install a fan heater. The combination of air circulation and heat will make a world of difference in balancing out the humidity.

- **Ventilation:** Sometimes, a humidity problem is caused by poor air circulation. Attaining a balance in ventilation may help you balance out the humidity. It can be as simple as opening a window or installing an HVAC system.

- **Dehumidifiers:** The surest way to keep the humidity level at the desired level is to install a dehumidifier in your growing room. This is particularly important if you grow many plants and you're concerned about excess humidity levels. Choose the most convenient for the size of the room.

How to Increase the Humidity for Your Houseplants

In the cold winter months, the humidity level in your indoor garden is likely to drop to very low levels, which can be bad for your plants. Many indoor plants are originally from a naturally humid environment. Therefore, they need an optimal relative humidity level of between 40-60% to stay healthy and will not survive properly in dry conditions.

To create the ideal living environment they need, you must take steps to increase the humidity. In addition to measuring humidity levels with a hygrometer, there are clear tell-tale signs to look out for that indicate that your plants need more humidity. Some of the signs of low humidity include

- Yellow or browned leaf edges
- Wilting and dropping
- The leaves feel crispy and dry to the touch

If your indoor garden plants are showing these symptoms, low humidity could be the problem. You should verify the humidity level by measuring it with a hygrometer and comparing your humidity measurement with the moisture needs of your plants. If you discover that the humidity level is too low, the following are some steps you can take to increase the humidity level.

Misting

Spraying plants with water will raise the humidity level around the plant temporarily. Note that you cannot use this method for all plants. Plants with hairy leaves such as Purple Heart and African Violets should never be misted. The "hair" on their leaves will retain water, which can lead to the harboring of harmful microorganisms and cause diseases.

Use Pebble Trays

Put a layer of pebbles in a tray and pour water into it until the pebbles are slightly covered, then place your plants on top. These pebbles will ensure that the plant stays above the water so the roots don't get too wet and rotten. The humidity of the room is raised as the water evaporates and adds moisture to the air.

Create a Microclimate

This process replicates the natural habitat in which plants grow in the wild. Placing all your plants together in a group creates a microclimate that helps to lock water in. You can also set a dish of water at the center to boost the humidity further.

Use a Humidifier

Humidifiers add water to a room's air automatically. The extra moisture they add to the air is great for plants as well as for people. But be sure to monitor the moisture level at all times, so the humidifier does not raise the humidity level to excessive levels. Using a unit that automatically detects the humidity level and shuts off when it's above the desired level will make this much easier.

Place Plants in Humid Rooms

You don't necessarily have to alter the humidity level of a room before you can plant houseplants. There are areas of your home such as the kitchens, laundry rooms, and bathrooms where the humidity is often high. Rooms like these are particularly great for water-loving plants that thrive better in high-humidity environments.

At the end of the day, when it comes to giving your plants what they need, experience will be your best friend. As you start growing your plants, you need to be observant and pay attention to how they respond to certain conditions – and be ready to make changes when necessary. There is hardly a one-hat-fits-all approach to maintaining moisture and temperature levels. You just need to monitor your plants continually and make changes as necessary.

Chapter 6: Indoor Pollination

If you can still remember a bit of basic information about plants from your elementary biology class, you'll recall how plants need to be pollinated to produce fruit. In the open, plants depend on insects like bees to collect pollen from the male flowers and transfer them to female flowers. The pollen sticks to the bee's body as it collects nectar and is then transferred by the bee to other plants.

The natural process of fertilizing flowers (pollination) is necessary for plants to produce fruit (and the seeds inside them). Aside from insects, pollen can also be carried by animals that come in contact with the flower or through wind and water. But all of these methods are unlikely to work in an indoor environment. This is why the question of pollination is one of the most common questions beginner indoor gardeners ask. Do indoor plants need to be pollinated? If they do, how exactly is this possible, given that the significant pollination mechanisms are not readily available indoors?

Why Is Pollination Important?

Most people would rather not have insects around indoors, from the annoying ones like flies and bugs to dangerous ones like spiders and mosquitoes. But while we'd rather have a world without them, insects are more important than we can imagine. We could say that our very survival hinges on them due to their role in pollination.

Pollination is one of the most important processes in nature, especially when it comes to growing food crops. We also need pollination for seeds to develop, even in plants whose fruits are not edible. Without pollination, the planet will be in trouble.

The transfer of pollen between the male and female flowers of plants of the same species leads to fertilization, producing fruit and seeds. Up to three-quarters of staple crops and one-third of all food crops need to be pollinated.

While it is possible to manually pollinate crops (and even compulsory in the case of indoor gardening, as you will find out), hand pollination is not an exact science. The accuracy of the process is limited, which makes it quite an unpredictable undertaking.

Bees are the most popular pollinators because of their wax and honey production. They are responsible for pollinating food crops worth $19 billion per year in the United States. While many other insect pollinators like ants, wasps, butterflies, and moths do their part, they're not quite as popular as bees.

How to Pollinate Indoors

It is possible to produce tomatoes, cucumbers, peaches, pineapples, and other food crops in your indoor space. Even less likely plants like corn can be grown indoors. But how is this possible if the most well-known pollinators are not present in an indoor garden?

As an indoor gardener, pollination is one of the most important things you need to learn about. Note that pollination is not always necessary. If your indoor garden is just for leafy plants or flowers, you don't need to learn much about it. But if you are producing certain indoor vegetables or fruit, or if you want your plants to produce seeds to grow new ones, you have to master indoor pollination.

Plants can be grouped into two categories based on how they are pollinated: self-pollinating or cross-pollinating.

Self-Pollinating Plants

Many indoor plants like tomatoes are self-pollinating. Such plants don't need pollen to be transported from one flower to another in order to bear fruit (tomatoes are actually fruit by botanical definition).

The flowers of self-pollinating plants are typically hermaphroditic (they have both male and female reproductive parts). This makes it easier to produce seeds and fruit. Examples of such self-pollinating plants include

- Beans
- Lettuce
- Peas
- Pepper
- Tomatoes
- Eggplants

Most self-pollinating plants don't require any attention at all as far as fertilization is concerned. But some of them can use a little help to increase the efficiency of the pollination process. This can be as simple as turning on a simple oscillating fan to produce a slight breeze. This will create the draft needed to help these plants self-pollinate more often. You can also give the plant a little shake now and then or tap the flowers lightly to achieve the same results.

Cross-Pollinating Plants

Unlike self-pollinating plants, cross-pollinating plants need all the help they can get for fertilization. Their male and female flowers are separate. But the pollen still has to find its way from the male flower to the female flower for pollination to occur.

In nature, cross-pollinating flowers rely on bees and other insects to pollinate them. But since indoor spaces are usually a no-bee zone, you have to step in to pollinate these flowers manually. There are a couple of ways to get this done. These include:

Let in a Breeze or Use a Fan

Again, the easiest way to ensure that the transfer of pollen between flowers takes place is by opening the window to let some breeze in or by positioning a fan to point toward the plants. The breeze will most likely cause some pollination to occur. While this is a simple solution, there are certain things to keep in mind if you're using this approach.

This method is recommended for windows during the spring or summer season.

- Be sure not to leave the plant at the window all day.

- Consider the lighting requirement of your houseplant. If your plant is affected by too much direct sunlight, then this method may not work for you.

- Make sure it isn't too windy outside. Strong winds can push your plants off the windowsill, cracking the pot or breaking off the plant stems.

If going the fan route, turn the fan on to a low speed and let it blow in a single direction consistently (instead of oscillating). Ensure the fan speed is not so high as to break off the plant stems or damage them.

Try a Vibrating Device

You can use an artificial pollination device such as a "Be the Bee" Pollinator to induce pollination. These devices are designed to be used directly on houseplants like strawberries and tomatoes. The vibration of their bristles will move pollen to the part of the flower where it needs to go. Devices like this can potentially increase the yield of your plants.

If you don't have a device like this, you can use an electric toothbrush as a make-shift pollinator. But ensure that the device is new and clean. Also, if you have anyone with a pollen allergy in your house, you must be careful when using devices that agitate pollen in this way.

In the absence of an electronic vibrating device, you can also shake the plant manually. To do this, gently shake the flower or the entire plant. This can be done daily to improve the chances of pollen release. Be sure not to roughen up your plant; firm but gentle shakes are recommended.

Manual Pollination

Opening up a window or using a vibrating device may not be enough to pollinate indoor plants with separate male and female flowers. For plants like this, you will have to actively pollinate them by taking the pollen from the male flowers and placing it onto the female ones.

The hardest part of this chore is actually identifying which flowers are the male ones and which ones are females. This may be difficult for someone that isn't familiar with flower anatomy. The structure of flowers also varies from one type of plant to another. However, you can simply look up information and photos online to understand what male and female flowers look like. Here are a few helpful tips that can help you with this identification:

- Male flowers often appear first before the female ones

- Male flowers are the ones with the stamen, and while the female flowers have a stigma, you can check photos of how this is supposed to look.

- In some plants, male and female flowers look distinctively different, making it easier to tell them apart. Most female flowers have a base that contains what will become fruit. In cucumbers, for instance, the female flowers look like baby cucumbers with beautiful yellow flowers at the end.

- If you inspect male flowers closely, you will notice something that resembles dust on their surface. These are pollen grains.

- In many plant species, male flowers are often smaller than females

Using all of these differences in quality, you should be able to tell the difference between male and female flowers. Now you can take some of the pollen using a cotton swab or small brush, then transfer it to the female flower.

An alternate method involves removing the male flower entirely from the plant, peeling back the flower petals, and rubbing the anther with the pollen still on it directly onto the female flower's stigma. The first method is generally preferable since you won't have to destroy any male flowers in the process. The flower can still produce more pollen which can be used to pollinate other female flowers.

Selective Pollination

If you are self-pollinating, you can get a bit more deliberate by making specific decisions about the type of plant you choose to breed. This sort of selective breeding involves combining the genes of two plants with desirable traits, such as bigger fruit or more flowers.

Selective pollination also helps you eliminate plants with weak genes in your indoor garden. You don't necessarily have to be an expert botanist or genetic engineer to do this. You simply have to watch your plants as they grow and note the ones with appealing qualities. Then when it's time to cross-pollinate, select the ones with the qualities you desire in their progeny.

Of course, don't expect to create a crazy new hybrid with incredible qualities through selective pollination in your indoor garden. This takes years of study and several rounds of pollination. Also, cross-pollination does not directly affect the fruit produced immediately, just the seeds and the future generation of plants produced from the seeds.

How to Tell if Your Pollination Effort Is Successful

Despite your best efforts, it will not be possible to tell immediately if your attempt to pollinate your plant or aid its natural pollination manually is a success or not. How long it will take for the plant to start showing changes varies from one plant to another. But if the pollination is successful, the flower's petals will wilt and drop, and fruit will soon begin to develop at the base of the flower.

But even if the pollination is not successful, the flower will still wilt and drop off, but no further development will occur. At this point, it will be too late to attempt another pollination. A failed pollination does not affect your plant itself. It will continue to grow until the next flowering cycle when you have the opportunity to try again.

All of these may feel like trial and error at first. But as you continue to pollinate your indoor plants, you will gradually become more familiar with the process and how much pollen the flower needs for fertilization.

Chapter 7: What Goes into the Pot?

Container gardening is the most common way to do indoor gardening, although it is often used outdoors too. Barrels, tubs, hanging baskets, boxes, and pots of different sizes serve both aesthetic and functional purposes in indoor gardens. Their practicality and ease of placement mean you can easily move them anywhere and make use of even the smallest patch of sunlight on your windowsill, balcony, on the ground, or even hanging on a wall.

There is no limit to what can be grown in a container of sufficient size. Different types of herbs, leafy vegetables, and even trees can continually grow and even thrive in a well-planned garden pot. You can use a single large container for just one plant or several smaller plants. Small pots can also be arranged in clusters, each featuring dwarf evergreens, annuals, perennials, or pretty much any other type of house plant you'd like to try.

What Type of Pot Works Best?

Nearly anything can be used as a container for your house plants, from bowls to baskets, boxes, old boots, old shoe tacks, barrels, and, of course, pots. As long as it is large enough to contain enough soil, has a flat bottom, and has adequate drainage holes, it is suitable. It all comes down to your creativity and personal preferences.

Of course, your choice of pot may also depend on factors like the type of plant, how much space you have, and the conditions in your indoor garden environment. For instance, while small pots are great for shallow-rooted plants, you will need a tall container for deep-rooted plants or small trees, while trailing plants and vines are perfect for a hanging basket.

Another factor to consider is the material the container is made from. There are different types of material, each with its unique features that determine their functionality and the limits on where they can be used. Here are a few of the different kinds of pot materials.

Clay Pots

Clay pots are known for their porosity which allows air to pass through them quite easily. This makes them perfect for keeping the roots of plants cool. They tend to have a flat base, and their weight makes them sturdy, so there is a limited risk of them tipping over. The only problem with clay is that it can break easily if it tips over or is impacted with sufficient force. Also, because of their porosity, the soil's water dissipates more quickly; you may need to water them more often. Drought-tolerant plants do well in clay pots.

Stone/Concrete Containers

Concrete or stone containers are not as fragile as clay pots, but they are comparatively quite heavy, which can make placement a bit of a challenge. Once put in place and filled with soil, moving them out of that position may be difficult. Hence, they may not be ideal for an indoor growing room where conditions vary widely. They are also not quite as porous as clay pots. Stone containers are ideal for growing tree plants and small shrubs.

Glazed Ceramic Pots

If you prefer something with a bit more aesthetic flair, then a glazed ceramic pot would be worthy of consideration. But they tend to be quite expensive and come in typically smaller sizes. This favors placement but also means you may not be able to grow large or deep-rooted plants in them. They are also quite fragile, so they must be placed in a stable position where there is minimal risk of tipping over.

Wooden Containers

Wooden boxes are typically made of cedar wood because it is more durable and pest-resistant. But they can be made from different types of wood as well, except treated wood (because of the risk of chemicals seeping from the wood into the soil). When using wooden containers, the interior should be lined with a plastic liner. This helps to prolong the life of the container, as wood tends to break down over time. You can also paint the exterior of the wooden container to extend its life further.

Other Types of Plant Containers

• **Metal pots:** Metal pots are great for displaying different types of plants. But they are prone to rust and may also get too hot under certain conditions. Instead of planting directly into them, you can place plastic containers inside the metal.

• **Polyresin Containers:** These are lightweight and cheap. But they are often flimsy and can be easily tipped over by the wind. Hence, they are best positioned on the floor. Despite their lightness, polyresin pots can still be quite durable.

• **Fiberglass Pots:** This is another lightweight alternative to conventional gardening pots. But they are thin-walled, which means there is less insulation for your plant.

• **Plastic Containers:** Plastic containers are also great for indoor planting. They can be used on their own but are often placed in another container. They tend to hold the moisture in, so you must be careful when watering your plants. Use a UV-protected plastic material as those are less susceptible to cracking when exposed to the sun.

• **Polystyrene Pots:** Polystyrene comes in a wide range of sizes and designs, making them a great choice for decorative houseplants. They are lightweight but still provide sufficient insulation for plants. But their weight also means wind could be a problem.

These are some of the most popular choices as far as indoor gardening pots are concerned. Of course, there are other non-conventional options such as repurposed materials like shoes, plastic pots, old shoe racks, etc. Whatever pot you choose, the most important thing is to make sure your garden plant will grow properly in it and take specific precautions regarding placement, drainage, and watering.

Layers That Go into a Pot

After picking out your container, the next question to answer would be what goes into it. Plants grown in pots need the best possible soil they can get. They also need sufficient aeration and must be properly drained if you want them to grow healthily.

Regular garden soil should not be used inside a garden container. It is simply too heavy and can easily become waterlogged, leading to root rot and a wide range of diseases and pests. Instead, what is known as a soilless mix should be used. Compost can also be used either alone or combined with a soilless mix.

Soilless mix is organic matter such as wood, peat, chips, perlite, and vermiculite. Slow-release fertilizer is also included. But it does not contain sand, silt, clay, and other inorganic matter.

Components of Soilless Mixes

Sphagnum Peat Moss

This is the most prominent component of most soilless mixes. Peat moss is slightly acidic, with a pH of about 5.8 for most products. It is lightweight, well-drained, and also water retentive. But until it is well-moistened with water, the particles will remain dry and dusty.

Bark

Tree bark is often added to the mix to provide airspace and improve drainage. It also reduces water retention. Mixes that contain bark are not great for starting seeds. They are best used for mature plants that prefer to dry out between watering.

Coir

Coir has similar properties to peat. It provides good drainage for the mix but also has great water-retention properties. It is now commonly used in place of peat moss in many mixes.

Perlite

Perlite is a volcanic mineral. It is an inert material that does not contribute any nutrient to the soil or affect soil PH. Perlite only enhances drainage and boosts water retention. Other examples of inert materials that may be used include polystyrene beads and calcined clay.

Vermiculite

The purpose of vermiculite in a soilless mix is to help hold water and nutrients in the mix. This is a silicate material that has been heated to increase its water retention capacity. This is particularly important for mixes used for growing seeds as it helps to lock the moisture in place long enough for the seed to germinate. There are different types or grades of vermiculite. The type used for home plastering or insulation is not suitable for use in potting mixes. The best place to purchase vermiculite will be at your local gardening center or the gardening section of a store.

Sand

A small quantity of sand may be added to add some weight to the mix and fill large pore spaces between the particles without impairing drainage. Often, coarse sand or sand derived from granite is used.

An ideal mix would usually contain about 40% peat moss, 20% pine bark, 20% vermiculite, and 20% perlite or sand.

Fertilizer in Soilless Mixes

While a soilless mix is great as far as aeration and drainage are concerned, it offers very little in the way of natural fertility. Thus, you may need to add your fertilizer, lime, and other materials to the mix to give your plants the nutrient they need.

Many soilless mix products may contain what's called a "starter charge" of fertilizer. It is usually enough to satisfy your plant's nutrient needs for a few weeks. But for long-term fertility, you have to add liquid or granular fertilizer to the mix regularly. You may also mix in slow-release fertilizer. This provides a constant supply of the needed nutrients for your plants as they grow.

Soilless mixes typically have a nominal supply of trace elements, so a fertilizer with sufficient micronutrients is recommended. A good number of commercial mixes also contain lime to keep the pH stable. Soilless mixes only need to have a slightly acidic pH to perform effectively. So, you don't need a lot of lime in the mix.

Pot Drainage

One of the most important factors when growing plants indoors is drainage. Proper drainage is necessary to ensure that the roots of your plants don't rot. Your garden pot is expected to have a drainage hole at the base to allow excess water to flow out. Good drainage helps to keep plant roots aerated, which is essential for the plant to grow healthily.

Gravel's Function

Adding a layer of gravel to the bottom of a planting container has long been recommended for container gardening. But this advice is more of a myth than an accurate fact. This erroneous advice may hurt your plant rather than help it. Having gravel at the base of the pot takes up room that would normally be filled by soil. This reduces how much soil your plants can make use of. But the most dangerous effect is on the drainage of the pot. The layer of gravel at the pot's base does not allow water to pass through as quickly as it should. Thus, the soil in the pot is likely to become saturated with water, which is bad for plant roots. Additionally, gravel adds unnecessary weight to the container, making it more difficult to move around.

What's the Alternative?

Potting soil alone is actually enough to give proper drainage for potted plants. You can also place a paper coffee filter at the pot's base before filling it with the soil mix. This prevents the soil from spilling out at the bottom of the container while still allowing water to pass through.

Additional Tips for Indoor Garden Potting

- The bigger the pot, the better. This is especially significant for large plants or if you want to grow more plants in a single pot. The roots of most plants need sufficient room to grow. Smaller containers may not retain enough water to get your plant through hot, dry days.

- Clay pots and ceramics are usually the most attractive options if aesthetics is important to you. Plastic pots are not so attractive, but they are great at retaining moisture and better than unglazed terracotta containers. You can also place a plastic container inside a larger clay pot.

- Be wary of black-colored pots. They absorb heat in the sun and will lose water faster than brightly colored pots.

- Most potted plants have to be watered often (about twice per day). Double potting is a strategy that can help you keep your plants cool, especially through hot summer days. It involves placing a smaller pot inside a larger one. The space between them should be filled with crumpled newspaper and peat moss. The filler material should also be watered when you water the plant.

- Hanging baskets are a great way to economize your space. You can grow leafy vegetables, herbs, tomatoes, and strawberries in them. They are also easy to tend and harvest when positioned at eye level.

- Containers that can be easily moved are great candidates for container gardening.

- Potted plants need to be fertilized regularly too. You should feed your plants at least twice per month with fertilizers. You can also add compost or fish emulsion occasionally to add some trace elements to your pot mix.

- Garden containers should be placed to get good ventilation and meet the light conditions best for the type of plant you are growing.

Chapter 8: Simple Indoor Greens

Leafy greens are a perfect candidate for indoor gardening. They are better grown indoors, where they are less likely to be destroyed by bugs and other pests. This chapter will mention some of the most common leafy green vegetables that are good for indoor gardening.

Also known as vegetable greens or salad greens, leafy greens are derived from a wide range of plants, but all are similar in terms of their nutritional composition and cooking methods. There are more than a thousand species of plants with edible leaves in this category.

Leafy greens are typically short-lived herbaceous plants. They constitute an important part of a healthy diet because they are packed with essential nutrients such as minerals, vitamins, and fibers. Leafy greens are known to reduce the risk of conditions like obesity, high blood pressure, and heart disease.

Growing your leafy vegetables indoors means you always have access to a fresh supply of these beneficial veggies, which can be eaten raw as a salad, cooked as a side dish, or in conjunction with the entrée, and included in several recipes.

How Much Light Do You Need for Indoor Leafy Green Gardening?

Leafy greens typically need about five hours of direct sunlight. But they will grow even faster if they can get more. Although a bright window would work fine, grow-lights are often recommended. Leafy greens grow better under consistent lighting conditions. Using artificial light can also help trick them into a longer harvest since you get to maintain an illusion of perpetual spring conditions.

What Type of Planters and Soil Should You Use?

Leafy greens grow better in nutrient-dense soil with a consistent moisture supply. Self-watering planters are an excellent choice for growing leafy greens. They are designed to slowly deliver water to your garden soil, keeping it consistently moist. Typically, they have a reservoir that you need to fill with water about once a week. You can also water the plant directly.

Leafy vegetables can also be grown in hydroponics. Some vegetables, such as lettuces, will grow better (nearly twice as fast) when they're grown hydroponically. Growing veggies hydroponically involves using no soil, just a coarse base material to anchor the roots and a steady supply of nutrient-infused water. Pretty much any leafy green can be grown this way. But it can be a bit complicated to manage and can be a little expensive.

Harvest Timing and Other Tips for Growing Leafy Greens

Leafy greens should be grown in a high-quality soilless mix or compost. Once your seeds germinate, you should turn on the lights daily in the morning and shut them off in the evening. The soil should be watered every couple of days if you are watering manually, as soon as the top of the planting mix feels dry. After about ten days, you can add a weak solution of fish emulsion and seaweed to the mix every week to supply micronutrients.

When growing leafy greens, you must keep them well-watered and maintain an ample supply of nutrients. Once the plants start to grow, you should also thin them regularly. Thinning can begin about three weeks after germination or as soon as two or three sets of leaves start to show. Plants growing closer than one inch apart from each other should be snipped above the soil level (don't uproot, so you don't disturb the soil). The snipped seeding can be used in salads or soups.

More active harvest can begin as the plants grow bigger. How soon you can start and the frequency of harvest depends on the specific vegetable. Harvest should start with the outer leaves while the rest are left to continue growing. For bulk harvests, you can clip greens throughout the container using fingernail scissors. But leave the growing tips so that another crop can be produced.

After about five weeks of growth, you should be able to get a robust harvest, enough to prepare two plates of salads three or four times per week. Harvest can continue like this for about six weeks.

As plants grow, you should raise your lights so that the plant doesn't get scorched by the heat. As a general rule of thumb, the light should be positioned at about four inches above the highest growing leaf in the cluster.

15 Leafy Green Plant Varieties You Can Plant Indoors

Spinach

Spinach is one of the most recognizable leafy greens that is grown indoors. The rich and hearty flavor of fresh spinach offers a delicious addition to salads, whether in cooked or raw form. Spinach is relatively easy to grow indoors in a pot. It is one of the easiest green vegetables to grow indoors.

Spinach does not need much sunlight, so you can easily grow it on a windowsill without artificial lights. A small pot six inches deep is enough to grow spinach. It can also be grown along with herbs and annual flowers.

Spinach is a cool-season crop, but it grows well even in the tropics and sub-tropical climates. It can be grown as a biannual crop (except during the hot summer months). All you need to provide is a cool space with enough water and the right soil temperature.

In warm weather, spinach will bolt very early and will start to produce seeds. However, some heat-tolerant varieties are ideal if you live in a warm climate. They grow slowly and will not bolt very quickly because they are more tolerant of high heat and humidity. Your spinach greens are ready for harvest after about six weeks of growth, depending on the growing conditions.

Celery

This is another famous leafy green that commonly goes into salads. It is popular among those watching their weight and people on a vegan diet. Celery belongs to the same family as carrots and parsnips.

Celery is quite easy to grow. A pot or planter that's about eight inches deep is enough to grow this vegetable. But you must keep the soil moist and feed it regularly with fertilizer. Celery is a cool-season plant. It grows well in cool, well-drained, and fertilized soil. It does not need a lot of sunlight and will grow well in the shade.

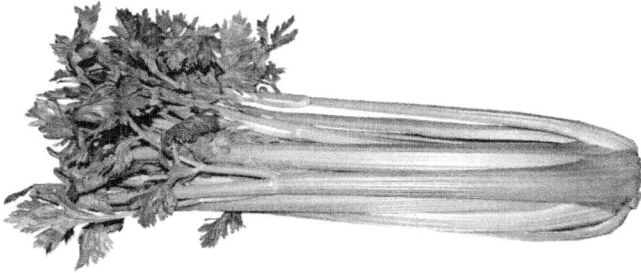

This vegetable is a heavy feeder. So, you have to fertilize the soil every 10-to-14 days using a balanced fertilizer. It also needs a constant supply of water (at least an inch of water weekly). Spreading a layer of mulch around the plant can also help lock the moisture in and keep weeds from growing. Although celery is a cool-season plant, extremely low temperatures can cause the plant to bolt early. Harvest can begin when the stalks are about eight inches tall. It can be harvested by snipping the stalks starting from the outside in.

Kale

Kale is another personal favorite of health enthusiasts. This vegetable adds texture and color to meals and also supplies beneficial nutrients. The thick green leaves are loaded with essential vitamins, minerals, and, of course, fiber.

Growing kale is easy. It can be grown indoors on your patio or balcony. Two kale plants can be grown in a 12-inch container. And it can be easily moved into the shade and out to the sun. If grown indoors under the right conditions, you may be able to enjoy a fresh supply of this leafy green throughout the year.

Kale is a cool-season crop that grows well under moist, fertile conditions. It can be grown in spring and fall, as it can tolerate frost. A rich and well-drained soil is the perfect growing soil for this plant. It also needs at least six hours of light every day. The plant should be kept well-watered. You can also apply mulch around the plant to lock in moisture.

Kale has shallow roots, so care must be taken when uprooting weeds around it to avoid damaging the plant. They are heavy feeders, so you need many nutrients (especially nitrogen) for them to grow properly. Harvest can begin when the plant is about 20–25 cm (8–10 inches) long, starting with the outer leaves.

Chards

Chards are a close relative of beetroots. They have glossy green leaves on leafy stalks, both of which are good to eat. The delicate baby leaves can be tossed with salads, while more mature leaves are often used as separate vegetables. The stalks can also be added to stir-fries for an attractive crispy addition.

Chards grow best in full sunlight, so they must be placed in well-lit areas or under artificial lights for about 6-to-8 hours every day when direct sunlight is not possible. Chard needs organically rich fertile soil and should be kept as moist as possible. The soil should be well-drained. They grow best in cool climates and can tolerate frosts to a moderate extent. But they will bolt quickly when exposed to an extremely low temperature for too long.

Chards need plenty of moisture to develop good-quality roots. Applying a layer of mulch to the soil can help conserve moisture. Chards also need a sufficient supply of both micronutrients and macronutrients. Fertilizer can be applied at planting and then at subsequent intervals. The leaves can be harvested at any point since both young shoots and mature leaves can be eaten. If the harvest is being done at maturity, the outer, fully developed leaves should be removed first.

Endive

Along with escarole, endive belongs to the chicory family. The plant has curly leaves with a prickly texture and a slightly bitter flavor. Escarole, on the other hand, has broad flat leave with a bitter and nutty flavor. Endives are typically harvested during summer, so early growing is recommended. They are best grown in excellent conditions but will tolerate minor temperature fluctuations.

This is primarily a cool-season plant that grows best when the days are short. The plant will perform better when planted in loose, fertile soil (preferably loam with good drainage). It can be placed in full sunlight or partial shade. Endives tolerate light frost but will bolt early if the weather is warm. The plant should always be well watered and shaded from extreme direct sunlight.

The outer leaves should be tied around the head about a week before harvest to keep the endive from developing a bitter flavor. You can also cover the whole plant with a box or pot to blanch. After blanching, a sharp knife should be used to cut the entire head. Early harvest is recommended if the weather is too hot or you are anticipating a hard frost.

Collard Greens

This cruciferous vegetable is a close relative of the kale plant. It is common in many southern delicacies mainly because of its crunchy texture and sharp taste, so it is often used to add flavor to otherwise bland meals.

Collard greens grow better in partial lighting conditions. They can be placed on the windowsill but should be moved to a more shaded spot on a hot summer afternoon. They are good with about six hours of sunlight daily. Collard greens are primarily cool-season crops that grow best in moist conditions. It can be grown both in spring and fall. They are strong and can tolerate hard frost.

The plant grows best in rich, moist, and well-drained soil. The soil should be kept evenly watered. Adding some mulch around the plant can help conserve moisture. Collard greens have shallow roots and should be carefully handled. The soil should be rich in nitrogen and other essential nutrients for optimal development. Harvesting can begin about two months after planting this vegetable, starting with the mature outer leaves. The leaves are sweeter if harvested after some frost.

Nasturtium

The Nasturtium plant has a pretty appearance with colorful blooms. It is easy to plant as it thrives under the poorest of conditions. But apart from being a pretty sight in the garden, this delicate salad green is also edible.

All the nasturtium wants is full access to the sun and an ample water supply, and it will grow healthily. It grows well in sunny spots in the garden but can also be grown indoors. There are climbing varieties of this plant that can be trained with vertical support.

Nasturtium plants need ample sunlight (10-12 hours per day) to grow properly. They should also be sheltered from the wind, which makes indoor growing perfect for them. They prefer free-draining soil, but soil fertility is not necessary. In fact, overly fertile soil will only result in a lot of leafy growth with no flowers. Once sown, there is no need to fertilize the soil.

The leaves, flowers, and even the seeds of this plant are edible. They are best picked while the plant is still young. The flower is often used as a colored garnish in salads and other uncooked dishes. The leaves are also added to the salad to give it a peppery taste.

Lettuce

Lettuce is a crispy leafy green preferred for its abundance of nutrients. Except for the Iceberg variety, it is rich in vitamins, minerals, and fiber and is often recommended for kidney problems, nervous disorders, and other health issues.

Lettuce can be grown indoors in pots placed on the windowsill. The planter can be shallow but wide since the roots don't grow very deep. Lettuce is naturally a cool-season plant. It does not have any strict soil preferences, but good moisture retention and fertility are necessary. Lettuce will also perform better in alkaline soil than in acidic soil.

Lettuce doesn't need a lot of sunlight. Even the heat-tolerant varieties should be protected from sunlight as they will bolt early if not well-shaded. The fresh leaves of the lettuce plant can be harvested at about four weeks. For a good harvest, the soil should be fed with some organic fertilizer each time you harvest.

Bok Choy

Also commonly referred to as Pak Choi, Bok Choy is a delicious leafy green belonging to the cabbage family. It features glossy green leaves on long white stems. The leaves are rich in carotenoids, folate, calcium, and other nutrients. Bok Choy is a delicious addition to salads and coleslaw.

Bok Choy can be grown indoors quite easily. It grows well in partial shade and only needs about six hours of light per day. However, if you live in an area with a very cold climate, then the length of light exposure can be increased. Pak Choi is best grown in a well-drained potting mix that is rich in organic matter. The soil should have a loose and crumbly texture and have a great water retention capacity.

This plant grows best in slightly moist soil. It should be watered regularly. Never let the soil become too dry but don't overwater. Harvest of the tender leaves can begin after about 3-to-4 weeks of growth. Harvest should start with the outer leaves. If you're harvesting whole heads, then you should wait for 45-to-55 days.

Brussels Sprouts

The flavor-packed Brussels sprouts look like miniature cabbage, but they are not baby cabbages even though both plants belong to the same family. This vegetable is a common addition to salad platters and is known for its health benefits. It is rich in antioxidants, minerals, vitamins, and dietary fibers.

Brussels sprouts are cool-season crops, so they grow best during the spring and fall seasons. They thrive better in cool weather and are best planted in fertile and moist soil with good drainage. Brussels sprouts have high nutrient requirements and particularly need plenty of nitrogen. The soil should be replenished with organic matter regularly throughout the time the sprouts are growing. They are also quite sensitive to boron deficiency, which leads to small buds and hollow stems. Thus, boron should be introduced to the soil.

Brussels sprouts need about 1-to-1.5 inches of moisture per week, or the plants will start to bolt. Harvest can begin at about 90-to-180 days after planting, when the plant is about 2.5-to-5.0 cm (1–2 inches) in diameter. Harvest should begin with the older sprouts at the bottom.

Mache (Corn Salad)

Also known as corn salad, Mache has a sweet, nutty taste. The delicately flavored plant can be eaten raw like other salad greens but can be cooked as well. Mache is a cool-season crop, and it grows very fast. It can be ready for harvest as early as forty days.

Mache can be grown in a pot or box 6-10 inches deep and about twelve inches across. Corn Salad isn't a very demanding plant, so a lot of fertilizer isn't needed. Just a healthy, well-drained soil rich in organic matter is good enough to plant this vegetable. It does need a lot of water and should be watered daily, early in the morning. More frequent watering may be required if exposed to direct sunlight.

Mache is generally low maintenance with similar requirements to lettuce. Because the growing duration of this plant is relatively short, you may not need to apply additional fertilizer after planting. But if the soil is too poor, you can add some manure or compost to promote healthy growth. The leaves are harvested when the plant is at about three centimeters. The base can be left in place for subsequent growth and harvest.

Cabbage

Cabbage is one of the most versatile greens used around the world. This leafy green is known for its crunchy and peppery taste in its raw state.

Cabbage is relatively easy to grow indoors. It can be grown anywhere, although planting season may vary depending on the climate. A standard 12-inches-deep pot is often used for indoor growing. Cabbage is a cool-season crop. It grows best in cool and moist soil. For optimal growth, give the plant at least six hours of light daily.

Cabbage should also be evenly watered to ensure the heads develop tightly. Cabbage has shallow roots and is a heavy feeder. Fertilizers should be applied for optimal growth. The soil should be fertilized as the plant heads and new leaves start to develop. The plant is ready to harvest when the head has been fully formed, and it feels firm when squeezed. It is harvested by cutting the head from the stalk using a sharp knife. If the stalk is left in the ground, a smaller head is formed, which can also be harvested.

Sage

There are different varieties of sage plants, but the one that is most commonly used for cooking is Garden sage. This silvery green herb is a common ingredient in many Thanksgiving and Christmas celebrations.

Growing sage indoors is pretty straightforward. The herb is best grown in clay pots. They allow better air movement, which is particularly beneficial to the plant. This is necessary because the Sage plant does not like to sit for too long in wet soil, and the clay pots dry out more quickly than others. Watering should be done moderately and only when needed.

The herb can be grown from seeds or propagated using stem cuttings in a technique known as "layering." This method of propagation is often preferred because the plants mature faster than when it is grown from seed.

Sage plants are affected by high humidity. You should also avoid getting moisture on the leaves when watering. A buildup of moisture on the foliage will give rise to powdery mildew. Sage plants need at least 6-to-8 hours of light daily. They are best positioned near a sunny window or grown under artificial lights.

Beet Greens

Beet Greens is a leafy vegetable commonly cooked with onions, garlic, and olive oil or eaten raw with salads. This is one of the easiest leafy vegetables to grow. The plant is a cool-season plant grown using beetroots.

The Beet plant has a long growing season. It is quite tolerant of fluctuating temperature but is best grown in cool climates. The best type of soil to grow this vegetable is loose well-draining soil kept moist. Beets need adequate sunlight for optimum development.

The young greens are harvested for a salad when the plant is about 2.5–5.0 cm (1–2 inches) in height. For a more mature harvest, the plant can be allowed to grow to 15 cm (6 inches) in length. The plant's roots can be harvested as well, but this is done earlier (at 2.5 cm) if you're planting for the roots.

Turnips

Turnips are popular as a root vegetable, but the leaves are quite nutritious too and can be eaten raw or cooked. Turnip greens are rich in different vitamins, calcium, and folate; they are often used as a replacement for kale and spinach in different recipes.

Turnips can be grown in early spring for a summer harvest or grown in the summer for a late fall harvest. Turnips grow better in well-drained soil with a loose texture. This type of soil supports good root development, which the plant needs to grow optimally. Turnips grow better in full sunlight but can also be grown in partial shade. The plant should be watered evenly to keep the soil moist. Turnip greens are meant to be harvested when the plant is about 10 cm tall. If you're growing for roots, then only two or three leaves should be removed from each plant.

Malabar Spinach

Malabar Spinach has the crispy texture of lettuce and the milky taste of spinach. It can be used in soups and stir-fries but is mostly used to prepare salads. Malabar spinach is one of the few leafy greens that grow pretty well in the shade. It needs only about 4-to-5 hours of direct light for good growth. The plant should be placed at the warmest spot in your grow-room, with partial or full access to the sun. It is a climber, so you have to provide some form of vertical support for the twine to attach to. It can grow to as long as 10-to-15 feet.

Malabar spinach is not a heavy feeder, but the soil needs to have good drainage. Compost or manure should be added to the growing medium to increase its texture and drainage. Supplemental feeding is not needed if manure has been added at the beginning. But if manure was not added, a weak dose of fertilizer can be added.

Chapter 9: Herbs That Thrive Inside

Many herbs can thrive indoors, and you don't even need a spacious sunny room or grow-room for them. You can simply set a plant pot in the kitchen on your countertop or on the windowsill, and you're good to go. Growing your herbs right next to you in your kitchen also comes with an extra advantage as you can easily snip fresh herbs for your dishes quite conveniently.

Herbs can also be grown in a dedicated grow-room. The key to creating an indoor herb garden that thrives is to know which herbs do well indoors and ensure they have everything they need to perform optimally. In this chapter, we cover some of the things herbs need to grow optimally and some of the best herbs to consider if you are looking to add herbs to your indoor garden or start a new herb garden inside your home.

Light Requirements for Growing Herbs Indoors

Herbs can be grown with just natural light, under grow-lights, or by using a combination of both. If you're using natural light, the plant should be placed as close to the south-facing window of your home as possible (again, from the northern hemisphere point of view). As you already know, this window sees the most light for the longest periods, even during short winter days. Even herbs native to subtropical and tropical climates, like basil, oregano, rosemary, and bay laurel, are well suited for this scenario.

East and west windows can also be used to grow herbs. They don't receive as much light as the south window, but they can be used to grow plants like mints, chervil, and parsley. These plants prefer less intense light and grow better in cooler temperatures.

You may also grow herbs under grow-lights. They need the full spectrum of light, so your grow light should be fitted with white lights. While the lighting need may vary from one plant to the other, the general recommendation is to place them about four feet from the light source. Bright-light herbs need 12-to-16 hours of light per day.

Whether you are using natural or artificial light, be sure to keep an eye out for any indications that the herbs aren't getting sufficient light. These include smaller leaves, abnormally pale leaves and stems, unusually spaced leaf sets, and yellowing leaves.

Drainage Requirements for Indoor Herbs

Herbs don't need a lot of water to survive (definitely not as much water as most vegetables). All you need to do is keep the soil moist consistently. A small watering can or even a drizzle under the sink is mostly sufficient. Watch the leaves for any changes and reduce the water if necessary. Letting the herb sit in waterlogged soil will lead to rot and destroy the plant.

Clay pots offer the best drainage. The only downside to them is that they dry out too quickly, especially if you live in a dry climate or have dry seasons. Always make sure that your herb pot has a drainage hole at the base and use a potting mix with great drainage characteristics.

If you place your herb on your kitchen countertop or windowsill, be careful when you water it. The tabletop can be ruined if you let the plant pot drain on it. A simple way around this is to place a plastic, ceramic, or rubber saucer under the container to catch any excess water.

Temperature Requirements for Indoor Herbs

Most herbs will grow properly with normal indoor temperatures during the day. This means they can be grown all year round. As a general rule of thumb, if you are comfortable in your home, then your herbs are probably comfortable too.

Most herbs are good with some nighttime chill as long as they are kept away from the open windows. Some herbs like basil don't tolerate chilly air at all, and their leaves will droop and fade with just a few minutes of exposure to chilly winds. If your herb is placed on a windowsill, I recommend you move it away from the window during the winter and summer months when the weather is cooler or hotter than the average indoor temperature, and when drafts are caused by open windows.

It's safe to use air conditioning indoors with herbs in the house. But you have to be wary of the effects of low humidity, and water the herbs more often. Herbs are not very demanding compared to vegetables, but you should fertilize regularly to keep the soil fertile.

Like leafy vegetables, herbs can also be grown hydroponically (without soil, in a water-based medium). This ensures that nutrients and moisture are supplied directly to the root of the plant. They can be grown under the right amount of exposure to a grow-light if access to sunlight is not possible.

Types of Herbs That Can be Planted Indoors

Basil

Basil is one of the most popular herbs and is used in a broad range of cuisine. It is commonly paired with tomatoes in many recipes. Growing basil indoors is quite easy. The seeds or seedlings can be grown in rich organic potting soil in your kitchen or grow-room. It is a short-term plant, so you can expect to start harvesting the leaves after a short while. It will continue to grow for several weeks, after which the stem begins to grow woody.

Basil loves bright light and grows well in the heat, making it a perfect candidate for southern or western window placement. You can also grow it with artificial light. Because it loves warmth, basil will not do well in cool or drafty areas, especially during the cold winter month.

Bay Laurel

Bay laurel is a Mediterranean shrub whose flavorful leaves are often included as an ingredient in different stews and soups. The leaves can be used fresh or harvested and dried for later use. For storage, the leaves of larger plants should be used. Older trees also offer the strongest flavor.

Bay laurel is best planted in fertile quick-draining soil. Bay laurel also needs good air circulation. The best placement for this plant is close to the west-or-east-facing window. It does not need a lot of sunlight and can be grown with artificial lighting. A common pest of this plant is a scale that can grow on the leaves and stems. Watch out for them and take quick action to mitigate an outbreak. (You can check out chapter three of this book for instructions on how to take care of a scale outbreak organically.)

Chervil

Chervil is an annual plant known for its anise-parsley flavored leaves. It is an essential ingredient in many delicacies, soups, and sauces, including the famous Bénaise sauce. It is often used for soups with ingredients like potatoes, steamed carrots, and eggs. Fresh chervil leaves may also be included in salads or dressings.

The seeds are planted in moist potting soil. You should use a deep container because the root of this plant tend to grow quite deep and will need a lot of room to grow. Plants are best placed in a cool spot in your garden room with access to a moderate amount of sunlight. Fresh young leaves are often harvested and used immediately, so you may need to grow a new batch every few weeks to maintain a steady supply.

Chives

This thin spiky grass-like herb is quite easy to grow, which is why many call it the gateway herb. The onion-flavored herb is the special favorite of many chefs that include it in soups, salads, and garnish. They are seasonal perennials grown mainly in spring.

Chives are best planted in fertile and well-drained soil. The soil mix can include some organic fertilizer or healthy compost. After this, you may not need to fertilize the soil again. The planting soil should be kept moist and well-watered. Chives thrive best with full access to the sun, but they can be grown pretty much anywhere (preferably near a southern window if you are growing indoors).

To harvest, use scissors or garden shears to nip off individual leaves, beginning with the outer ones. The stalks left in the soil will resprout after a while for another harvest.

Mint

From peppermint to spearmint, chocolate, apple, orange, and so on, all the varieties of mint are quite resilient and can be grown both indoors and outdoors. The leaves and sprigs of this plant are often used for tea and drinks as well as salads. They are also attractive houseplants.

A healthy plant just needs a container of potting soil with good enough drainage. It can be placed in an area without direct sunlight but should be watered regularly to keep the soil moist. The plant should also be misted regularly to keep the humidity level optimal.

You should rotate the plant pot after every few days so that the plant does not bend toward the light. Mint does not need a lot of nutrients, but occasional fertilizer applications will not hurt.

Oregano

Oregano is a common addition in many Italian, Mexican, and Middle Eastern delicacies. It is a close relative of the mint plants. It can be used in both fresh and dried forms, although the dried leaves are more pungent than the fresh.

Oregano requires care and maintenance similar to other mint plants. The major consideration is to keep the soil moist to prevent the plant from drying out. It grows well in moderate to strong light and is easy to grow indoors.

Parsley

Parsley is often added to soups to boost flavor and brighten colors. It is also included in recipes for fresh sauces and salads. This herb is quite easy to grow. All you need is just good soil, a lot of light, and an ample supply of water.

Parsley can be grown from seeds, but you can also buy the young plant and grow it in a container with good drainage holes and organic potting soil placed in strong lighting. The herb will grow weak and spindly if it does not get sufficient light. The leaves can be harvested and used fresh or dried for later use.

Rosemary

Rosemary is one of the most commonly used herbs used in soups and sauces. It is beloved for its earthy fragrance. This plant grows best in full sunlight, and the brightest windows indoor can hardly provide as much sunlight as a sunny garden. But it can still be planted indoors by placing it close to a south-facing window or using artificial lighting.

Rosemary prefers hot and sunny areas and grows well in the summer months. But it will also survive and thrive in cooler temperatures as well as long as it has access to strong light. High humidity is always a problem for this plant as it is susceptible to powdery mildew under high humidity conditions. When grown indoors, you can use a fan to create a gentle breeze that helps to keep humidity levels under control.

Thyme

Thyme is both an aromatic and culinary herb. Its versatile scented flavor makes it possible to incorporate it into nearly any recipe. This tiny-leaved plant can be grown indoors with well-drained soil.

This herb is best planted in a fast-draining soil mix and placed close to the sunniest window in the room. It does not need a lot of water. You should only water the soil lightly when the soil is dry. A weak solution of liquid seaweed or fish emulsion should be used to fertilize the soil every two weeks.

Harvesting Herbs

Herbs can be enjoyed in various ways. You can harvest fresh herbs for use immediately or freeze and dry them for long-term storage and later use. Whether you are using fresh or drying for later, the best time to harvest herbs is right after the flower buds appear but before they open up. This is the time they have the highest concentration of oils and the strongest flavor.

The best time of the day to harvest herbs is early in the morning, just after the morning dew has evaporated from the surface of the leave but before the sun is high in the sky.

Freezing

One of the ways to preserve herbs for later use is by freezing. It preserves the essential oils, which gives the herbs their flavor. Freezing herbs as a method of preservation is quite easy. You simply have to rinse the herb, remove leaves from its stems, and leave them to dry out on a plate. Put the dried leaves in a plastic bag and place them in the freezer. The result is a clump of herbs that can be thawed and cut up when you need it.

An alternate method is to freeze the leaves individually on a flat tray first, then gather them up and place them in a plastic bag later. This method makes it possible to use individual leaves later if you wish to. You can also blend the herbs first and make them into a paste. This paste is then frozen in ice cube trays or a plastic bag. One advantage of this method is that you can make a blend containing different herbs and use them together.

Not all herbs should be stored in this way. Some herbs that can be frozen for later use include basil, chervil, cilantro, chives, dill, lemon ball, lemon verbena, lovage, mint, oregano, sage, thyme, savory, and rosemary.

Drying

Instead of freezing, you can dry your herbs for use later. This method is simple as well. All you have to do is tie small quantities of the herb together and hang them in a well-ventilated room. They should be air-dried away from the light. This should be done while the leaves are still on the stem. After drying, remove the leaves from the stem and store them in an airtight container.

Some herbs, such as basil and parsley, cannot be dried this way because they have thick, succulent leaves that will not dry quickly unless you live in an arid climate. Herbs like this are better dried in a dehydrator. Examples of herbs that can be dried include basil, dill, fennel, oregano, sage, savory, scented geraniums, and tarragon.

The truth is, growing herbs indoors is relatively easy, but many of them have peculiar requirements, especially regarding sunlight. But if you have artificial light and you water the plant properly, there should be no issues. The trick is to identify the best type of herbs to grow indoors based on the conditions available in your indoor space. Do your research about how to grow and care for a particular plant. You can start small, beginning with a few herbs at first (start with the easy to grow ones like thyme and parsley), then gradually work your way to the trickier ones like rosemary and lavender.

Chapter 10: Vegetables and Fruits

It's easy to imagine growing leafy veggies and herbs indoors. After all, they're small and can easily fit into a pot. But when you think of indoor plants, most fruits and large vegetables aren't likely to be top on your list. But you'd be surprised at the number and variety of fruit trees you can successfully grow indoors under the right conditions.

From citrus to peppers, peas, strawberries, squash, and even bananas, the list of not-so-conventional vegetables that can be grown indoors is endless. This final chapter will cover just a few of them.

Tomato

Most people consider a tomato a vegetable. But it belongs to this chapter because it is also a fruit. Tomato is actually one of the most popular indoor plants. There are different types and varieties that can be grown indoors, but the best types for indoor gardening are the smaller varieties because they can be accommodated conveniently in a pot. These are also called patio tomatoes. Other popular tomato varieties include:

- **Beefsteak Red:** This is a variety of tomato with large, brightly colored, and thick-fleshed fruit. The plants grow very large, so they have to be supported.

- **Cherry:** This variety produces a small fruit that is quite flavorful

- **Roma:** These types of tomatoes are egg-shaped. They are fleshy but not very juicy and are commonly used in sauces and pastes.

Patio tomatoes are the small hybrid tomatoes that are the most ideal for container gardening. The plant only grows to a height of about two feet. There are several varieties and hybrids of cherry and patio tomatoes that are small-sized and produce smaller fruit, making them easy to grow indoors. Examples include Sungold, Jellybean, Tommytoe, Supersweet 100, Pear, and Green Zebra.

Tomatoes can also be grouped based on how they fruit. The two broad categories of tomato plants based on this criterion are determinate and indeterminate. The former (determinate) produces all its fruit at once while the latter (indeterminate) continues to produce fruit over time. Either can be planted in an indoor garden, but you will need to repeatedly grow new seeds every month if you plant the determinate variety.

One of the factors that make tomatoes an ideal candidate for indoor gardening is how fast they grow. While their growing season is restricted to spring outdoors, they can be planted at any time of the year when grown indoors.

Soil

Tomatoes grow better in organically rich soil. The soil should be loose with a neutral to acidic pH. You don't need a special soil mix to grow tomatoes. A regular mix used for growing regular vegetables will work just fine for tomatoes.

Your potting container should be between 12-to-16 inches deep. But specific space requirements may vary depending on the variety of tomato you're planting (larger plants will need larger pots). The planting container should have good drainage holes so that the soil does not become waterlogged.

Planting

When you're growing tomatoes from seeds, they should be planted at a depth of about ¼ inch into the starting mix. You will need artificial grow-lights for an indoor tomato garden. A heat mat may also be used to help warm up the soil and help the seeds to germinate faster. Tomatoes can also be grown directly from seedlings in a small pot. Either way, the plants should be moved to a permanent container when they're about four inches in height.

One of the good things about growing tomatoes (which I already mentioned in the chapter on pollination) is that they are self-pollinating. However, you may aid the process by shaking the plant's stem gently when it starts to bloom. You can also transfer pollen directly from the male to female flower or place a gently oscillating fan in the area to blow the plant's pollen about.

Growing tomato plants indoors may be a bit problematic if you have pets. While the fruit is edible, the plant itself may be toxic to dogs, cats, and even people. Care must be taken to keep the leaves and stems from being ingested by the uninitiated.

Light

Naturally, tomato plants thrive in full sun. So, if you plan to grow them indoors, you have to make arrangements for supplementary light. You will need to ensure that the plant gets at least ten hours of direct sunlight every day, either by placing it in front of a sunny window or using artificial lighting. Poor sunlight will cause the stems to become weak and unable to support fruit. If you're using grow-lights, the light should be installed about one or two inches above the top of the plant until they begin to flower. There should be a mechanism to raise the light as the plant grows taller.

Water

While the tomato plant loves water, it is easily damaged by an excess of it. Maintaining a good moisture supply with proper drainage is recommended to prevent the root from rotting. Be sure to keep an eye on the container to see if it needs water, and water it if the soil feels dry to a depth of about an inch down.

Temperature, Humidity, and Fertilization

Tomatoes need a lot of nutrients which is why they are best grown in organically rich soil. You should also add slow-release fertilizer to the soil to feed the plant. The simplest part of growing tomatoes indoors is that you don't have to bother about temperature. They grow well at average room temperature. Humidity is also not a problem for an indoor tomato plant.

Carrots

Another common indoor plant is the carrot. In fact, it is easier to grow carrots in an indoor garden than in a conventional outdoor garden. This is mainly because carrots prefer a steady supply of moisture which is usually difficult to provide outdoors during hot summer days. In an indoor garden, you can maintain an ample supply of water to help the plant thrive.

Soil and Potting

Growing carrots indoors also allows you to grow varieties of different sizes and colors that are not very common in grocery stores. Growing carrots indoors is surprisingly easy. They can be grown in a container in any room of your home under the right conditions. Containers of any size can be used for growing baby carrots. But for the longer varieties, you will need to get deeper pots (about eight inches deep for the short ones and up to twelve inches deep for standard-length carrots).

Carrots need good-quality potting soil to grow. They can be grown from seeds or regrown using the top of the carrots. The seeds should be started directly in the planting pot since the roots don't respond well to being transplanted.

The plant should be placed on a sunny window to get an ample supply of water or under a grow-light. The grow-light should be kept at a distance of about three inches from the seedlings and adjusted as they grow.

The surface of the soil should be kept moist at all times. When planting carrots indoors, you should be vigilant and ensure you monitor the water regularly. Outdoors, the plant can make do with watering about two inches per week. But you will need more for an indoor garden.

Carrots can be harvested at any time as soon as they show a mature color. The tiny immature ones make a tasty treat, too, so they can be harvested as well. Be careful when harvesting, as disturbing the soil can affect the other carrots.

Peppers

There are different varieties of peppers that can be grown in indoor gardens, but chili peppers are the most popular option. They are fun to grow and very easy too. Peppers thrive well outdoors, but they can also be grown indoors. Another advantage of growing them indoors is that they can double as decorative plants because of their vibrant colors.

Water and light are the two most important resources you need for growing peppers in a container. Pepper plants need at least five hours of direct sunlight daily, but they can be grown in artificial light as well. They grow better when they get an ample supply of light. The plant should be watered frequently (at least once a day or more, depending on the temperature) but not too much, as this can cause root rot.

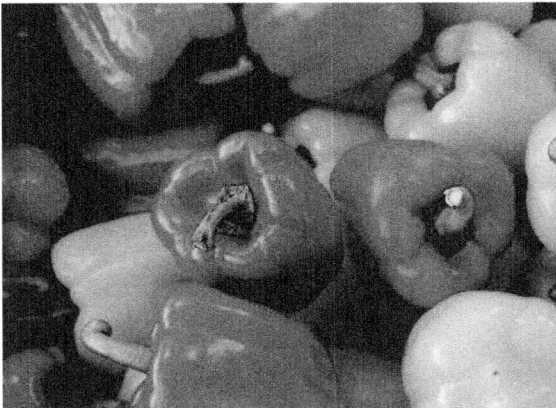

Smaller pepper varieties are better suited for indoor growing. They should be planted in good quality soil with high organic content and good drainage. That last bit about drainage is important since waterlogged soil will damage the plant. The soil should be fertilized with compost or a slow fertilizer once a month.

Like tomatoes, pepper plants are self-pollinating, so you don't need insects to produce fruit. But you may assist the process by hand pollination or simply shaking the stem gently to help distribute the pollen.

Strawberries

Most people find growing strawberries indoors even better than growing them outdoors for a lot of reasons. Indoor growing gives you greater control over the temperature, lighting, and moisture conditions than you would get in an outdoor garden. Your strawberries are also safer from pesky critters.

There are different varieties of strawberries that can be grown indoors and different ways to grow them. The two major types are the June-bearing strawberry plants (so-named before, they only fruit in June) and the ever-bearing variety that can produce fruit more than twice in a year.

The Alpine strawberry plant is the best variety to grow indoors because it is not easily affected by a lack of space like other varieties are. You can grow strawberries in a pot placed on your windowsill in any room of your house, or in your dedicated grow-room.

One common precaution to take when you're growing this plant indoors is to avoid overcrowding the space. Strawberries are susceptible to diseases (especially mold issues), and overcrowding can increase the risk of mold developing and spreading.

Strawberry plants also need a lot of sunlight. Your plant needs to get at least six hours of sunlight per day, either directly from the sun or artificial light.

The root system of this plant is quite shallow, which means it can grow in pretty much any container. All it needs is good soil, sunlight, and the right amount of water. Slow-release fertilizer should be added to the soil at least once a month to supply essential nutrients (especially nitrogen) until the plant starts to flower. Fertilization should be done routinely every ten days once flowering begins.

You should check your strawberry plants daily to ascertain if they need water or not. You should water (to a depth of 2.5 cm) as soon as the top feels dry. Strawberry plants like water, but an excess will damage the plant.

Oranges

Like many of their other citrus relatives such as lemons and limes, oranges can be grown indoors. They can be planted in a large pot on your patio or in your grow-room. While citrus trees are larger than your regular indoor plants, they are relatively easy to grow. As long as the clay, plastic, or ceramic pot is large enough to contain the plant's large root balls, and other conditions are right, you are good to go.

Specific dwarf varieties are your best bet for indoor growing. Oranges need sufficient sunlight to grow. At least eight hours of daily sunlight is recommended. They don't have a dormancy phase like many other plants, so keeping the light on at all times is recommended.

Oranges grow best in acidic soil. The soil should have great drainage and have some loam in it. There are specific potting soils for citrus trees available in many home- improvement and gardening stores. Buying one of these will be a convenient alternative to formulating your own mixture. Like other plants, you should maintain the moisture at an optimal level by watering the soil as soon as you notice it is starting to dry out.

Conclusion

One thing is clear from what we have covered in this book. There is an indoor gardening option for everyone. It does not matter what your living situation is, the size of your space, or how much sunlight you get daily, as indoor gardening can be customized in different ways to suit your specific situation.

Whether you want to grow vegetables, herbs, or tree crops, you can either modify your existing conditions or look for plants that are more likely to grow in your space. The possibility of using different creative potting techniques also allows you to maximize limited space and still get impressive results. You can turn a corner of your kitchen into a thriving garden or transform a wall or windowsill into a green space to nurture a wide variety of plants.

At the end of the day, it's all up to you. As long as you can find a spot that gets plenty of light or you are willing to invest in artificial grow-lights, you can create ideal lighting and temperature conditions to grow delicious greens.

But the most important thing you'll need to grow indoor vegetables successfully is your willingness to get serious about it. At the end of the day, what plants need most of all is someone to give them the care and attention required to thrive. The big question to ask yourself is whether or not you are ready to put in the work to start growing your own vegetables and plants indoors.

Rest assured the effort will be well worth it. Good luck and happy gardening!

Here's another book by Dion Rosser that you might like

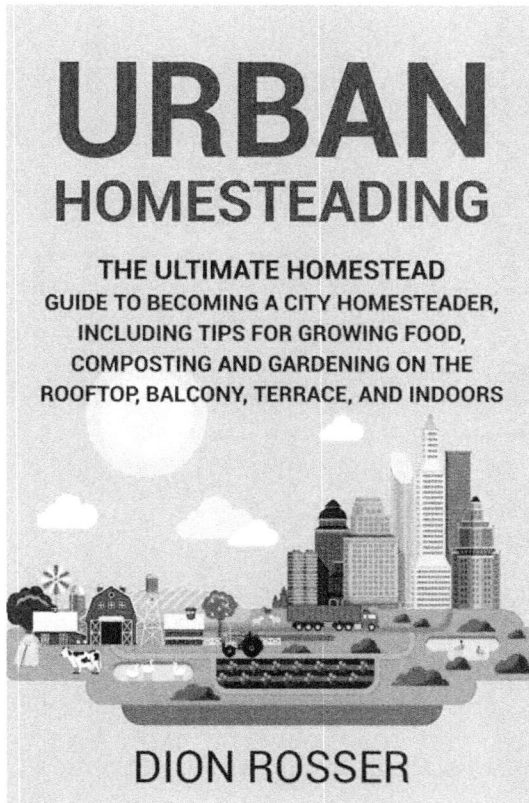

URBAN HOMESTEADING

THE ULTIMATE HOMESTEAD GUIDE TO BECOMING A CITY HOMESTEADER, INCLUDING TIPS FOR GROWING FOOD, COMPOSTING AND GARDENING ON THE ROOFTOP, BALCONY, TERRACE, AND INDOORS

DION ROSSER

References

admin. (2021, May 16). 32 Best Green Leafy Vegetables to Grow in Containers. Retrieved from Balcony Garden Web website: https://balconygardenweb.com/best-green-leafy-vegetables-in-containers-salad/

Bawden-Davis, J. (2016, April 4). All You Need to Know About Organic Fertilizer. Retrieved from Pennington.com website: https://www.pennington.com/all-products/fertilizer/resources/what-is-organic-fertilizer

Benefits of Indoor Gardening - 8 Top Benefits. (2020, January 8). Retrieved from Indoor Gardening website: https://indoorgardening.com/8-benefits-of-indoor-gardening/

Davis, S. (2020, September 18). 7 Science-Backed Benefits of Indoor Plants. Retrieved from Healthline website: https://www.healthline.com/health/healthy-home-guide/benefits-of-indoor-plants#7-benefits

Editors, T. (2018, August 13). Everything You Need to Know About Container Gardening. Retrieved from Good Housekeeping website: https://www.goodhousekeeping.com/home/gardening/a20707074/container-gardening-tips/

Epifano, M. (2020, June 9). The Best Indoor Garden Ideas for Bringing the Great Outdoors Inside. Retrieved from Apartment Therapy website: https://www.apartmenttherapy.com/15-indoor-garden-ideas-for-wannabe-gardeners-in-small-spaces-228575

Everything You Need To Know About Lighting. (n.d.). Retrieved from The Sill website: https://www.thesill.com/blogs/plants-101/lighten-up

Exchange, H. (2020, July 20). Tips For Growing Herb Plants Indoors. Retrieved from The Herb Exchange website: http://theherbexchange.com/tips-for-growing-herb-plants-indoors/

Extension Web Support. (2019, May 29). Here's the scoop on chemical and organic fertilizers. Retrieved from OSU Extension Service website: https://extension.oregonstate.edu/news/heres-scoop-chemical-organic-fertilizers

Extension, I. (n.d.). *What Makes Plants What Makes Plants What Makes Plants Grow Grow Grow? ? ?* Retrieved from website: https://edis.ifas.ufl.edu/pdf%5C4H%5C4H36000.pdf

Farm, C. (2020, May 8). 6 Expert Tips to Create a DIY Indoor Garden. Retrieved from Cornell Farm website: https://cornellfarms.com/blogs/houseplants/6-expert-tips-to-create-a-diy-indoor-garden

Gibson, M., & Russell, E. M. (2020, February 10). Organic vs. Non-Organic Gardening: A Comparison. Retrieved from Gardening Channel website: https://www.gardeningchannel.com/organic-vs-non-organic-gardening-compared/

Grant, A. (2021, June 21). StackPath. Retrieved from www.gardeningknowhow.com website: https://www.gardeningknowhow.com/edible/fruits/strawberry/strawberry-plants-indoors.htm

How to Grow Herbs Indoors. (n.d.). Retrieved from Bonnie Plants website: https://bonnieplants.com/gardening/how-to-grow-herbs-indoors/

How to identify common houseplant pests. (2017, August 11). Retrieved from HOMESTEAD BROOKLYN website: https://homesteadbrooklyn.com/all/2017/1/17/common-insects-pests-on-houseplants

How to Pollinate Your Indoor Fruit and Vegetable Plants. (2019, August 12). Retrieved from IGWorks website: https://igworks.com/blogs/the-igworks-indoor-gardening-blog/pollinating-your-indoor-fruit-and-vegetable-plants

Hughes, M. (2020, September 10). 4 Tips for Choosing the Best Containers for Your Houseplants. Retrieved from Better Homes & Gardens website: https://www.bhg.com/gardening/houseplants/care/containers-for-houseplants/

Iannotti, M. (2021, August 17). Use These Tips to Grow Vegetables Indoors. Retrieved from The Spruce website: https://www.thespruce.com/how-to-grow-vegetables-indoors-1403183

Indoor Plant Pests: Bug Identification & Control. (n.d.). Retrieved from Planet Natural website: https://www.planetnatural.com/pest-problem-solver/houseplant-pests/

Jauregui, R. de. (n.d.). How to Raise the Humidity of an Indoor Garden. Retrieved from Home Guides | SF Gate website: https://homeguides.sfgate.com/raise-humidity-indoor-garden-20964.html

Laura. (2019). Gardening Under Grow-lights | Gardener's Supply. Retrieved from Gardeners Supply website: https://www.gardeners.com/how-to/gardening-under-lights/5080.html

Lebbanister, M. (2013, September 27). Temperature and the Indoor Garden - Part 1. Retrieved from Homegrown Hydroponics website: https://hydroponics.com/temperature-and-the-indoor-garden-part-1/

LIPFORD, D. (2009, December 24). How to Grow Houseplants in Artificial Light | Today's Homeowner. Retrieved from Today's Homeowner website: https://todayshomeowner.com/how-to-grow-houseplants-in-artificial-light/

Lisa. (2018, May 29). Simple Ways to Pollinate Indoor Plants. Retrieved from The Practical Planter website: https://thepracticalplanter.com/how-to-pollinate-indoor-plants/

Mast, J. (2018, November 9). How to Increase the Humidity for Your Houseplants. Retrieved from Bloomscape website: https://bloomscape.com/plant-care/how-to-increase-the-humidity-for-your-houseplants/

Merkham, D. (2014, July). The Importance of Pollination | Chicago Gateway Green. Retrieved from Chicago Gateway Green website: https://www.gatewaygreen.org/the-importance-of-pollination/

Nickleson, L. (n.d.). Growing Tomatoes Indoors (Is It Worth It?). Retrieved from Juice PLUS+ website: https://www.towergarden.com/blog.read.html/en/2016/9/growing-tomatoes-indoors.html

Old Farmer's Almanac. (2020). Grow Your Own Salads Indoors All Winter. Retrieved from Old Farmer's Almanac website: https://www.almanac.com/grow-your-own-salads-indoors-all-winter

Reilly, K. (2020, February 28). Your Ultimate Guide to Growing Herbs Indoors. Retrieved from EatingWell website: https://www.eatingwell.com/article/289996/your-ultimate-guide-to-growing-herbs-indoors/

Rhoades, H. (2021, April 26). StackPath. Retrieved from www.gardeningknowhow.com website: https://www.gardeningknowhow.com/garden-how-to/projects/an-indoor-garden-how-to-diy-indoor-garden-room-ideas.htm

Temperature for an indoor edible garden. (2021, January 17). Retrieved from Northern Homestead website: https://northernhomestead.com/temperature-for-an-indoor-edible-window-garden/

Tilley, N. (2019, May 30). What Makes Plants Grow: Plant Growing Needs. Retrieved from Gardening Know How website: https://www.gardeningknowhow.com/special/children/how-plants-grow.htm

Tilley, N. (2021, July 26). StackPath. Retrieved from www.gardeningknowhow.com website: https://www.gardeningknowhow.com/special/containers/choosing-containers-for-potted-environments.htm

Vanderlinden, C. (2021, August 21). How to Grow Tomatoes Indoors. Retrieved from The Spruce website: https://www.thespruce.com/growing-organic-tomatoes-indoors-2539817

Vinje, E. (2012, December 10). How to Plant in Pots - Container Gardening. Retrieved from Planet Natural website: https://www.planetnatural.com/container-gardening/

Volente, G. (2019, July 27). How to Pollinate Indoor Plants. Retrieved from Greenhouse Today website: https://www.greenhousetoday.com/how-to-pollinate-indoor-plants/

Walliser, J. (2019, January 4). Houseplant Fertilizer Basics: How and When to Feed Houseplants. Retrieved from Savvy Gardening website: https://savvygardening.com/houseplant-fertilizer/

Weisenhorn, J., & Hoidal, N. (2020). Lighting for indoor plants and starting seeds. Retrieved from extension.umn.edu website: https://extension.umn.edu/planting-and-growing-guides/lighting-indoor-plants

Whitman, A. (2020). Best Herbs for Growing Indoors | Gardener's Supply. Retrieved from Gardeners Supply website: https://www.gardeners.com/how-to/herbs-indoors/8920.html

Why Grow Organic? (n.d.). Retrieved from Organic Growers School website: https://organicgrowersschool.org/gardeners/library/why-grow-organic/

Yares, K. (2016 7). What Is Organic Gardening? Retrieved from pender.ces.ncsu.edu website: https://pender.ces.ncsu.edu/2014/04/what-is-organic-gardening-2/

Yares, K. (2021, June 14). StackPath. Retrieved from www.gardeningknowhow.com website: https://www.gardeningknowhow.com/special/organic/five-benefits-of-growing-an-organic-garden.htm

Zimmer, F. (2020, April 2). Do Indoor Plants Need Pollination. Retrieved from Indoor Plants for Beginners website: https://www.indoorplantsforbeginners.com/do-indoor-plants-need-pollination/

Printed in Great Britain
by Amazon